# Dynamite Kites

Second Edition

30 Plans to Build and Fly

*For Cory Robert Wren, with love*

—S.L.C.

# Dynamite Kites <sup>Second Edition</sup>

## 30 Plans to Build and Fly

### Jack Wiley and Suzanne L. Cheatle

TAB BOOKS Inc.
Blue Ridge Summit, PA

SECOND EDITION
FIRST PRINTING

Copyright © 1988 by TAB BOOKS Inc.
First Edition copyright © 1984 by TAB BOOKS Inc.
Printed in the United States of America

Library of Congress Cataloging in Publication Data

Wiley, Jack.
Dynamite kites.
Includes index.
1. Kites. I. Cheatle, Suzanne L. II. Title.
TL759.W54   1988     629.133'32      87-33606
ISBN 0-8306-2969-6 (pbk.)

Questions regarding the content of this book
should be addressed to:

Reader Inquiry Branch
TAB BOOKS Inc.
Blue Ridge Summit, PA 17294-0214

Front and back cover photographs courtesy of Into The Wind, Inc.

# Contents

# Preface to 2nd Edition

This second edition is a condensed version of *The Kite Building and Kite Flying Handbook*. The instructions for each project have been shortened, and a set of general instructions is included. Illustrations for framing and for patterns are provided for each project. In some cases, variations of framing, tail, and bridle arrangements are included. Also included are illustrations of each finished kite, with bridle and tail arrangements.

The introductory material is condensed into three chapters and arranged in a logical order. It is my hope that this new arrangement will make the book easier to use, and result in greater enjoyment to those who wish to get involved in this venerable and entertaining hobby.

—Suzanne L. Cheatle

# Introduction

Building and flying kites has long been a popular hobby and pastime, dating back to ancient China. Today it is enjoying a popularity that is essentially worldwide.

I was first introduced to kite building and kite flying as a small child when my grandfather made kites from wooden sticks, string, paper, and rag tails. Then came the fun of flying, thrilling to the magic of a kite staying aloft by the power of the wind.

At a young age, I started making kites of my own. Early on, I learned that some performed better than others, and as time went on I began to learn some of the principles of kite design. From basic two-stick kites, I advanced to more elaborate constructions.

Over the years, I have never lost the fascination of designing, building, and flying kites. Quite the contrary, my interest and enthusiasm have grown.

Many interesting manufactured kites are now available, some at low prices, and most people begin, usually as children, with one of these kites. They provide an easy introduction to the world of kite flying.

For many people, kite flying never goes beyond using ready-made or manufactured kites. This, of course, can be an interesting recreational activity in itself, but I feel that the real excitement of kites is to go beyond this stage to designing, building, and flying your own kites.

There has long been a need for a handbook that focuses on the how-to aspects of kite building and flying. This book is an attempt to meet this need.

All of the kite plans shown are for kites that are flown on string from the ground. While kites that carry small payloads (such as message-drop kites) are included, man-carrying kites (such as those pulled by land vehicles and boats) are beyond the scope of this book.

An important feature of this book is the complete plans and instructions for making a variety of kites. Some of these are very old and proven designs;

others are more recent innovations. Some are easy to make, some are more difficult. The selection was made to provide different types and designs of kites for all levels of interest and building skills. No prior knowledge of kite building or kite flying is presumed.

You might soon want to design and construct your own original kite designs. The information and projects included in this book will provide you with a solid background for doing this. Information has been included on the aerodynamics of kite flying and how to design kites.

Closely related to kite building is kite decorating. Painting and decorating kites can become an art form. Part of Chapter 3 is devoted to decorating kites.

This book focuses on kite building and kite flying as a hobby, but the information should also be helpful to those who want to go into custom-building kites to sell or establishing kite stores, which are now popular in many parts of the United States and other countries.

It might seem that all possible kites have been designed and constructed, but this does not appear to be the case. Major new designs have appeared in recent years, and others are almost certain to follow. Kites, like sailboats, never seem to run out of potential. Both are very old endeavors, yet hundreds of years and thousands of minds applied to the task have not exploited all of the possibilities. Even more, the amateur has a chance for a piece of the action with kites. Unlike space travel, for example, the amateur with limited funds can design and invent new kite forms. Even more, he can construct them and try them out—all on a limited budget.

This book gives you the information you need to do it yourself. It is a how-to book. By that I mean that it is intended as more than just something to be read. This book gives the information that is required for doing it yourself, but most of the learning will come from actually building and flying the kites. This book will guide the way, but keep in mind that you must not only read this book, you must also get involved with actual kite building and kite flying.

While much of the material in this book comes from my own kite building and flying experiences, many other people along the way shared their ideas and techniques with me. Thus, it is impossible to acknowledge all the help given for the compilation of this book. To the many people who freely shared their ideas and experiences, I would like to extend a sincere thanks.

Jack Wiley

# 1
# Kite Facts

A *kite* is a heavier-than-air device that is flown on the end of a string, line, or rope and is kept aloft by forces created by wind pressure.

Although traditional kits featured a framework of sticks of wood, bamboo, or other materials, some modern kits have no framework at all. These kites are known as *flexible kites*. One example is a parachute-like device that is flown on the end of a string.

Balloons or inflatable devices that are flown on the end of a string only qualify as kites if they are heavier than air.

A few words must be said about kite size and purpose. Most of us have seen, if not in person then on television, man-lifting kites that are towed by a land vehicle or boat. Although these are kites in the real sense of the word, they are mentioned here only from a historical perspective. This book details how to make and fly small kites, with you on the ground holding the kite string, and the kite in the air. Our only concern with very small payloads, such as with message-drop kites.

It is difficult to define exactly what is meant by *small kites*. There is a natural temptation to make kites a little bigger, and a little bigger, and then a little bigger yet. The kite construction detailed in this book is limited to kites on string that can be flown by one person, although records for size of kites flown by more than one person are discussed.

## TYPES OF KITES

Kites come in many shapes and forms, but most belong to one of three basic types or are some combination of these: flat kites (with or without bows), box or cellular kites, and semirigid and nonrigid kites.

## Flat Kites

Flat kites consist of a flat framework with a cover of paper, cloth, plastic sheeting, or other material. This appears to be the most ancient form of kite, yet it remains popular. Flat kites usually require a tail to give them stability. Stability also can be achieved on some flat kites by adding a keel, or by adding an arch or bow to them, which allows them to be flown without tails or keels. Although the idea of using a piece of string to bow a kite is generally credited to William Eddy, many earlier kites had achieved this effect from the force of the wind bending the wings as the kite was flown or from using slightly curved sticks.

A primary attraction of flat kites is the many possible outline shapes that can be used, including geometric figures, insects, people, birds, and abstract shapes. Flat kites also make excellent surfaces for designs and pictures.

## Box, or Cellular, Kites

Box, or cellular, kites are three-dimensional. In general, they allow greater lift and stability than is generally possible with flat kites. They can be constructed in many different shapes and sizes, with or without winged surfaces, keels, and so on.

## Semirigid and Nonrigid Kites

Semirigid and nonrigid kites were developed mainly in the United States, starting in the 1940s. The main types are the parawing or delta wing, the sled, the parachute, and the parafoil. These designs have added an exciting new dimension to kite building and flying.

## Other Types

Some kite designs cannot be neatly classified as flat, box, semirigid or nonrigid. *Balloon kites*, for example, are basically air-filled kites. The air is used to give the kite shape and form. In use, they often take on characteristics of one or more categories of kites. Small kites made of folded paper often take on characteristics of both rigid and semirigid kites. *Rotary kites*, essentially propellers or wind spinners, do not fit in any of these categories. There are also kites rigged like sailing ships, and others shaped like gliders and airplanes, that are difficult to place in specific categories.

## HOW KITES FLY

A basic understanding of how kites fly and the basic principles of their design will provide a foundation for designing, building, and flying kites.

There are two fundamental concerns to designing kites: functional and aesthetic. Both are important, but only the functional concerns, based on the laws of aerodynamics, determine if and how well a kite will fly or perform.

In fact, attempts to make kites more aesthetically appealing often reduce performance. A figure kite, for example, might perform less well than a simple geometric shape, and a painted design on the covering of the kite could add weight and reduce performance.

The flying performance of a kite depends not only on its design, construction, and rigging, but also on the conditions under which it is flown (wind, temperature, and so on) and the skill and technique by which it is flown.

## Basic Aerodynamics

For our purposes, we will consider kites to be heavier-than-air devices (they weigh more than the volume of air they displace). Kites, thus, are *aerodynes*. In order to stay aloft on the end of the string, a kite must overcome the force of gravity. The force of the wind is used to accomplish this task.

## Lift

*Lift* is the component of the total aerodynamic force acting on a flying kite that is perpendicular to the relative wind and is normally exerted in an upward direction, opposing the pull of gravity.

Air is made up of particles that are constantly in motion and that resist the passage of any object through them. This resistance can be demonstrated by trying to rapidly move an object with a large surface area through the air. Air resistance can be felt as you try to ride a bicycle at high speeds; most of the energy applied to the pedals is used in an attempt to overcome air resistance.

Air resistance makes kite flying possible. Because the air resists the passage of the kite, the kite, when anchored or towed along on the end of a string and angled properly, is provided lift by the force of the wind. The air is deflected downward, taking the path of least resistance.

It is important to note that kites frequently fly in one place, with little or no forward motion. It is the wind and not the kite that is moving. The effect is the same. If the wind is 10 m.p.h., the effect is essentially the same as towing the kite along at 10 m.p.h. on a calm day. If the wind is 5 m.p.h. and the kite is towed at 5 m.p.h. in a direction into the wind, the effect is essentially the same as flying the kite in a 10 m.p.h. wind or towing the kite along at 10 m.p.h. on a calm day.

It's the *relative wind* that is important in kite flying. We will assume that, unless otherwise stated, the kite is flying on a fixed length of string anchored on the ground, as would be the case when you are holding the string on the ground without moving your position, letting string out, or taking string in. In this case, the relative wind is the same as the actual wind. The relative wind is how the kite "sees" the wind.

This concept is extremely important to the aerodynamics of kite flying. If a bicycle rider moves along at, say, 10 m.p.h. on a windless day, he feels the relative wind. It is essentially the same thing as being motionless, say, on a stationary exercise bicycle and facing a 10 m.p.h. wind.

The fact that the kite remains relatively stationary while the air moves simplifies the problem of understanding kite flight. Everything becomes much more complicated when the object, a sailboat for example, also is moving. Because the sailboat has motion in a certain direction, the relative wind (the wind that affects the sailboat) can be quite different than the actual wind.

In the case of the kite, it's the kite that stays still. The air rushes against the kite.

It is helpful to consider the kite as an inclined plane. Assume that a kite is aloft and is ''flying'' in one spot. The wind is a constant 10 m.p.h. The kite weighs 6 ounces and is heavier than air. The kite stays aloft by shoving the air down with its bottom surface and pulling the air down with its upper surface after the air has passed over the forward edge of the top of the kite. The kite makes the air go down. In exerting this downward force upon the air, the kite receives an upward counterforce. The principle involved is known as *Newton's law of action and reaction:* for every action there is an equal and opposite reaction.

Air is actually quite heavy. A cubic yard of air weighs about 2 pounds at sea level. As the kite pushes air downward, it gets an equally hefty upward reaction, which keeps the kite up. If the kite pushes the air down, the air must push the kite up. The kite is thus an inclined plane, an air deflector.

*Bernoulli's theorem* says that at the same time as air passes below a wing, air also passes above it, but since the air on the topside moves a longer distance over the curved surface of the wing, it moves faster and reduces the pressure above the wing. The air below the wing moves more slowly, which increases the air pressure below the wing. This principle was discovered by Daniel Bernoulli, a Swiss mathematician, in 1738. In the case of the kite, it is then the change in the relative pressures above and below the kite that causes the kite to lift.

Now, back to our 6-ounce kite that is staying aloft in one place in a 10-m.p.h. wind. For this condition to exist, the downward force upon the air would be 6 ounces, the same as the upward force upon the kite. The kite is in a state of equilibrium. The sum of all acting forces is zero.

If the downward force upon the air becomes more than 6 ounces, the upward force upon the kite also becomes more than 6 ounces and the kite moves upward, or climbs.

By the same token, if the downward force upon the air becomes less than 6 ounces, the upward force upon the kite also becomes less than 6 ounces, and the kite drops downward, or sinks.

This is a very basic and practical way of viewing how a kite remains aloft, climbs, and sinks. It also is useful for designing kites, as detailed later in this chapter.

Our discussion so far assumed that the wind was a movement of air more or less parallel to the earth's surface. In actual practice, however, this is not always the case. For example, there are updrafts of air, especially near mountains, that would serve to lift a kite. In most kite flying, updrafts probably play only a minor role. The strength of the wind and changes in the wind strength and/or direction are extremely important.

## Angle of Attack

Most kites must be at an inclined angle to fly. If, once aloft, a kite performs like an airplane or a glider with slack in the kite string, it is essentially an airplane or glider that used the kite principle to carry it aloft.

The kite is flown at an inclined angle so that as the air (by the force of the wind) passes it, the air meets the kite at an angle and is forced downward. The angle by which it is inclined in relation to the direction the air is moving toward it is the *angle of attack*.

In kite design and flying, the angle of attack is an extremely important consideration. Kites, by nature of their design, do not all use the same angle of attack for their best performance. Also, for a specific kite, the same angle of attack might not be best for all wind conditions.

On many kites, the flying angle also can be changed by making adjustments in the *bridle*, by adding or reducing tail, or by making other similar adjustments.

Because a kite is anchored to the ground by a string, it moves from the ground to the highest point of the flight in an arc, assuming that the anchor position is not changed and the length of the string remains constant. If the string remains perfectly straight from the point where it is anchored to the kite, the arc that the kite moves through depends on the length of the kite string. In this case, the angle of attack becomes less as the kite reaches greater heights, assuming that the kite remains at a constant angle in relation to the kite string. (In actual practice, the weight of the kite string may cause the string to curve downward as it leads up to the kite.) The angle of the kite in relation to the string might change, but the change in the angle of attack applies at least in a general way to many kites.

## Balance and Stability

To this point in our discussion, we have assumed that the kite has perfect balance and stability. The kite does not change its angle of attack by rocking forward and backward, nor does it twist or move from side to side. It does not stall or dive. In actual practice, however, most kites do not have perfect balance and stability. This situation is perhaps fortunate, since a perfectly balanced and stable kite flying only in a perfect arc at the end of the kite string wouldn't be much fun to fly. The thrill of a dragon kite, for example, would largely be lost if it didn't go through a lot of antics.

Still, in most cases a high degree of balance and stability is desirable for most kites. Balance and stability depend to a considerable extent on the design and construction of the kite. Some designs are inherently more stable than others. Balance and stability often also depend on the attachment and adjustment of the bridle strings.

Flat kites often require tails to give them adequate stability. The lift of a kite is affected not only by the weight of the kite, but also by *drag*, which is the resistance of the air to the forward and backward motion of the kite. Drag is in the directions that the kite moves, not the direction of the wind. The tail of a flat kite acts not only as a weight for balancing and stabilizing, but also, and perhaps most importantly, as a drag. The increased drag brought about by the tail as used on many flat kites does limit the maximum altitude that can be reached with any given length of string to less than that of many kites without tails, but this is generally a required sacrifice to give the flat kite adequate stability. Essentially all kite designs involve compromises.

Flat kites often can be bowed to give them adequate stability without the need for a tail. The performance of many flat kites thus can be improved.

The addition of one or more keels also can be used to give a kite greater stability. This method can be used on many kite designs, including flat and bowed kites, sled kites, and delta wing kites.

The flexibility of the cover material on many kites adds stability. The covering materials on many flat kites, for example, yield in the air pressure when they are flown, often forming curved surfaces.

The flexibility of the kite sticks or frames also adds stability. Many flat kites are actually bowed kites when flown because the outer edges bow back from the pressure of the wind, which explains why some so-called flat kites are able to perform so well without tails.

Box kites and other cellular kites often have better balance and greater stability than are typical of flat or bowed kites. There are a number of reasons for these features. Sections of the covering material are often perpendicular to the main inclined planes of the kite when it is aloft, serving in effect as keels or rudders. These kites typically have greater surface areas than do flat kites.

Balance and stability are often improved on box kites and other cellular kites by the addition of side wings. Keels are used on some box kites. Shaped wing surfaces also have been tried, but whether or not they significantly improve balance and stability is debatable.

Some of the modern semirigid and nonrigid kites of delta wing, sled, and parafoil designs have extremely good balance and stability. These designs were made possible by talented designers and inventors, and by the use of wind tunnels, computers, and modern synthetic materials.

## Wind

The wind is an extremely important variable in kite flying. A *calm* exists when wind is blowing at less than 1 m.p.h. Under this condition, smoke rises vertically or very nearly so. *Light air* is a wind of from 1 to 3 m.p.h. Under this condition, the direction of the wind can be detected by smoke, but not by an ordinary wind vane.

A *light breeze* is wind from 4 to 7 m.p.h. Under this condition, leaves rustle, ordinary wind vanes show wind direction, and you can feel the wind on your face. A *gentle breeze* is from 8 to 12 m.p.h. Under this condition, light flags are extended and leaves are in constant motion. A *moderate breeze* is wind from 13 to 18 m.p.h. Under this condition, small tree branches are in motion and loose paper and dust are raised. A *fresh breeze* is wind from 19 to 24 m.p.h. Under this condition, many small trees begin to sway. A *strong breeze* is wind from 25 to 31 m.p.h. Under this condition, large tree branches are frequently in motion, and umbrellas are frequently turned wrong side out. Of course, winds can get even stronger, but this is generally the full range under which kites are flown.

Some winds have a relatively constant direction over a period of time; others are variable. Wind that appears in gusts, for example, can make kite flying more difficult.

Like sailboats, kite performance varies with wind conditions. Some kites fly well in light airs and poorly in strong winds, and vice versa.

## DESIGN VARIABLES

The wind is an important variable in kite designing, construction, and flying. There are many possibilities. You can wait for favorable wind conditions, or you can design and construct kites for specific wind conditions. On a day when there is a light breeze, you can use a kite that is specifically designed and constructed for this condition. When there is a moderate breeze, you will use another kite, which is suitable for that condition. The kite built for a light breeze would probably be of lighter construction and might well break if you attempted to fly it in a moderate breeze. The kite built for a moderate breeze probably would be of much heavier construction, and it might not get off the ground with a light breeze.

Kite design involves working with a lot of variables. We will now take a look at some others.

## Shape and Form

A kite must have some shape and form. It could be a variation of some standard kite shape or form, or it might be an original shape or form. It might be a flat or bowed design, a box or other cellular design, or a semirigid or nonrigid design. The possibilities are almost without limit, at least until you begin to take flying performance into consideration. Then, kite aerodynamics must be considered.

## Construction

Once you have a basic kite shape and form in mind, the next step is to construct the kite. There are a number of considerations here. You will need to design the sticks and frame for the kite. The kite must have adequate strength, but at the same time it generally must have an absolute minimum of weight if it is to perform well. (You may want to skip the frame and design a flexible kite.)

After you have a basic frame for the kite, you will need to decide on a covering material. Again, you will be faced with the problem of adequate strength with a minimum of weight.

## Tails and Drogues

A tail does two basic things: it gives extra drag and it adds extra weight to the tail section of the kite. Both can add stability. A tail often can be the solution for a kite that uncontrollably loops and spins. The tail can increase stability by keeping the kite facing in the right direction and preventing the kite from twisting.

Tails are of various constructions, including strips of cloth tied at intervals to a length of string, and long strips of cloth, plastic, or crepe paper. In some cases, a single tail will be adequate; other kites require two or more tails.

A *drogue* is basically a wind cup. A drogue serves essentially the same purpose as a tail and, in many cases, can be more efficient than a tail. A drogue catches air in a manner similar to the way a sea anchor catches water.

## Bowing

*Bowing* is another important design possibility. Bowing can increase the self-righting tendency of a kite, thus increasing the stability. When the kite turns, the wind has a favorable angle to turn the kite back. This principle can be used for designing kites or modifying designs that turn out to be poor performers.

Bowing can be a smooth curve, an angle at the center of the kite, or angles elsewhere. The bowing can be slight or exaggerated, or anything in between. An exaggerated bow does tend to reduce the size of the lift surface.

## Venting

*Venting* is basically the addition of holes or openings in the covering material of the kite. Some box kites have more vented area than covering area.

Venting allows air to pass through the kite and escape. When properly done, venting can add stability to some kite designs.

## Other Design Variables

You also might want to experiment with a number of other design variables, such as rudders, airfoil-shaped surfaces, and tapering. Much can be learned about kite design from flying kites, both individually and in trains (see Chapter 3).

# DESIGN METHODS

There are many methods for designing kites. For example, kites can be designed in the imagination, on paper, or by trial and error. You make a modification on an existing kite, then you try it out. If it doesn't work, you try something else. Some kite designers are engineers and apply wind tunnels, computers, and modern materials to their kite designing. Other people take a more "backyard" approach.

There is no one way of designing kites. Amateurs on very limited budgets have made important contributions to kite design.

A growing number of kite artists design and construct kites as art objects rather than as flying objects. Kites can be nice to look at hanging from a ceiling, as well as flying on the end of a kite string. This does not mean, however, that a beautiful kite cannot be a good performer, too. Many kites are a blend of performance and beauty.

An important attraction to kite designing is that you are free to do it the way you want. If a kite design doesn't work out well, generally not much is lost, and you can always try again.

# 2

# Tools, Work Areas, and Materials

Only a few tools, a minimal work area, and readily available, inexpensive materials are required for you to get started in kite building. As you gain experience, however, you probably will want more and better tools, a better work station, and more elaborate and expensive materials. Inadequate tools, work areas, and materials can limit your ability to make interesting and functional kites, so you should try to have the best setup possible within the limits of your budget and interest.

If you are just starting out and have never constructed a kite before, you probably will want to keep expenses to an absolute minimum. You will want to take advantage of what you already have: a workshop in your garage or basement, for example. If you have built model airplanes or other related things, you probably already have many of the tools and materials that you will need for making kites. Start with what you already have and then add to your equipment as the need develops.

Since you may not have the essential items for getting started, a detailed list follows. Tools required for intermediate and advanced work, up to the level of making custom kites as a business, also are listed. A variety of work stations for various levels of interest and skills are covered. Materials described begin with common items and progress to exotic, space-age fabrics.

## TOOLS

A variety of tools are useful for kite construction work. As a general rule, quality tools are more expensive to purchase, but they are often the most economical in the long run, because cheap tools are easily broken or damaged under normal use.

# Knives

Three basic knives are suitable for kite construction work: fixed blades, folding blades, and removable blades.

**Fixed Blades.** Knives with fixed blades are available in a variety of shapes, sizes, and qualities. The handle can be of wood, plastic, metal, or other material. It is securely attached to the blade, often by means of rivets, in a fixed position. Carbon steel blades are best for kite construction work, although those of stainless steel are sometimes used. Carbon steel does rust unless it is lightly oiled or otherwise protected, but it holds its edge longer.

Although many utility knives with fixed blades can be used for kite construction work, those designed especially for modeling and wood carving wood are especially desirable.

Fixed-blade knives are generally the safest type to use. If properly constructed, there is little danger of the blade coming loose or folding up, which could cut your fingers. When you are selecting a fixed-blade knife, make certain that it feels comfortable in your hand. The quality of the steel used in the blade should be such that it will hold a fine cutting edge.

Fixed-blade knives do have some disadvantages, too. The blade of the knife can't be folded out of the way for carrying in your pocket. Also, you can't use more than one blade with the same handle.

**Folding Blades.** Pocketknives or clasp knives have blades that can be folded back into the handle for carrying and storage. Pocketknives are available with one or more blades and are easy to carry. Pocketknives are available in a variety of shapes, designs, and sizes. Useful blades include the clip, spear point, slant-tip, spey, and sheep-foot. Pocketknives with one or more of these blade types can be used for kite construction work. As a general rule, a pocketknife with one or two blades is preferable to a model with many blades since some of the blades on the latter type of knife will be off-center, and the knife will be wider and heavier, making it more awkward to use.

Pocketknives are available in a variety of sizes. Those in the medium size range are most useful for general kite construction work.

Although pocketknives are easy to store and carry, they do present the possible danger of snapping shut while they are being used and cutting fingers. For shop use, I prefer to use fixed-blade knives. Pocketknives, however, are useful for cutting string, making kite repairs, and so on when you are flying kites.

**Removable Blades.** Removable-blade knives are also suitable for kite construction. They offer the advantage of using a single handle for a variety of blade shapes and sizes. Make certain that the blades can be securely attached to the handles so they will not come loose while you are using them. Removable blade knives often are sold in sets with a variety of blade shapes and sizes. This type of knife can be very useful for kite construction work, especially when you are working with soft woods and other easy-to-cut materials.

**Sharpening Blades.** Regardless of the knives you select, you will want to keep them sharp. To do so, you will need an oilstone. A number of suitable oilstones are on the market, both natural and manufactured. Especially good are the Washita and Arkansas stones, both natural stones. It's a good idea to have a slab of each, because each has different honing characteristics. The coarser Washita oilstone can be used first, followed by the finer Arkansas oilstone. You can obtain these two stones together, with the Washita on one side and the Arkansas on the other. A number of other oilstones, with similar cutting characteristics, are available.

Small slabs of oilstone about 6 inches long and 1½ to 2 inches wide will suffice for most knife-sharpening work. You also will need a smooth leather stropping pad, the same as used for razors. A piece of smooth, genuine leather also will work. It can be tacked to a block of wood to make it more convenient to use.

A variety of other tools also can be used for sharpening knives, including grinding wheels and electric knife sharpeners, but it is easy to keep knife blades sharp and functional with an oilstone and strop alone.

## Safety Razor Blades and Razor Knives

Razor blades are extremely useful, but if you use one, make certain it is a safety blade with a metal guard over one edge.

Special knives with razor-type blades are available for hobby and modeling work. Some of the knives with removable blades feature razor-type blades. These will often serve in place of safety razor blades, although there are uses for both.

Razor blades and razor knives are useful for cutting softwoods and a variety of other materials used in kite construction. They are especially useful for cutting balsa wood.

## Chisels

Chisels are useful for some kite construction jobs. The Japanese-style carving chisels are handy for a variety of kite construction tasks. These chisels, when properly sharpened, have razor-sharp cutting edges that are ideal for notching kite sticks and other similar tasks. When you are working on wood spars for very large kites, larger wood chisels, such as those designed for carpenter or wood-carving work, are useful.

Like knives, chisel blades require frequent sharpening. Oilstones and strops can be used to maintain keen cutting edges.

## Saws

A variety of saws are useful for kite construction work. Extremely useful is a *coping saw* (also called *scroll* saw). It features a handle that is attached to a U-shaped frame, and a removable blade fastened in the frame. Many coping saws allow the blade to turn to various angles. Blades, which have ripsaw-type teeth, are available with various numbers of teeth per inch. A blade with 15 or 16 points to the inch is satisfactory for general kite construction work.

Although not essential for most kite-construction work, a *power jigsaw* or scroll saw can be very useful. This type of saw can be used for the same types of cutting jobs as a hand coping saw, but generally with greater speed and accuracy. A power jigsaw can be very useful for anyone who decides to go into custom kite making on a business basis.

Cutting large wood stock into small spars for kite construction work presents special problems. Although small ripsaws can be used, cutting accuracy can be a problem. Small, circular, bench power saws designed for hobby work can be useful here.

Larger circular *bench saws* can be used similarly, except that these generally have wider blades and take out a larger *kerf* (the area of wood removed by the blade) when sawing. The result is more waste wood when cutting small spars.

*Circular saws* permit a variety of cutting operations, including crosscutting, ripping, squaring, mitering, grooving, rabbeting, and beveling. Some of these cutting tasks are useful in kite construction work.

*Saber saws* are sometimes useful in kite construction work. A saber saw can be used to do cutting tasks similar to those done with a power jigsaw or scroll saw, but generally with less accuracy. Saber saws do have the advantage of greater portability, however.

*Hacksaws* are useful for a variety of tasks. They are available with traditional frames with handsaw-type or pistol grips, or with file-type handles. The file type can be used in areas where a regular hacksaw will not fit. Three basic teeth sets are available: alternate, raker, and wave. Although the hacksaw is primarily a metal-cutting saw, it also can be used to cut many other materials, including wood and a variety of hard plastics.

Hacksaw blades come with various numbers of teeth per inch. The choice depends on what metal or other material is to be cut. The blades are made from several materials, the most expensive being hard tungsten. This material works well for cutting hard metals. For most kite construction work, less expensive blades, such as those of molybdenum, will suffice.

A variety of other hand and power saws also can be used for kite construction work, including compass saws, keyhole saws, backsaws, and power band saws. Keep in mind, however, that kite construction generally involves working with small spars, so large hand and power tools are often awkward, if they can be used at all. Small tools designed especially for hobby and craft work are generally more suitable for kite construction work.

## Scissors and Shears

Scissors are used for a variety of cutting tasks in kite construction work, especially for cutting paper, thin cardboard, fabric, plastic covering materials, thread, and string. Scissors are available in a variety of sizes, designs, and qualities. Scissors of at least medium quality are recommended for kite construction work, since those of low quality dull quickly and are difficult to sharpen properly. Size is a matter of personal preference.

A good pair of scissors will last a long time when it is properly used and cared for. Cutting metals, wires, and similar hard materials will ruin most scissors quickly. There are other tools better suited for these cutting tasks.

Even when used properly, scissors eventually become dull. They can be taken to commercial shops for sharpening if you don't have the tools and know-how to do this work yourself.

Scissors should be kept clean and dry. If you get glue on the cutting blades, for example, clean it off before it has a chance to set.

A variety of shears or snips are available for cutting metals. Since various metals, especially soft metals, are sometimes used in kite construction, metal shears, especially small sizes, can be useful. The basic design is often called a *tinsnip*. Another type of shears, called *duckbill* or *aviation snips*, are useful for cutting curved patterns in metal. Special aviation snips are available for cutting left-handed. Combination aviation snips that can cut either way also are available.

As a general rule, small metal shears are most useful for kite-construction work, because you will generally be cutting thin pieces of aluminum, brass, copper, and other soft metals and alloys.

When they are properly cared for and used, metal shears will last a long time. Avoid cutting wire and nails, or you will quickly ruin the shears.

Metal shears eventually become dull. Take them to a commercial shop for sharpening if you don't have the tools and know-how to sharpen them yourself.

Metal shears should be kept clean and dry. Apply a small amount of oil to the pivot pin from time to time.

## Pliers

Various pliers are used for gripping and holding small items, and for cutting, stripping, and crimping. There are over 100 different types and sizes of pliers being manufactured, and it is important to select pliers carefully for maximum usefulness for kite construction work.

**Slip-Joint Pliers.** Slip-joint pliers are "regular" pliers. The jaws can be positioned for grasping small or large objects, and many slip-joint pliers feature a wire cutter at the base of the jaws. They are suitable for cutting soft nails and easy-to-cut wires. Slip-joint pliers, with or without wire cutters, are available in lengths from about 5 inches to 10 inches with various shapes of jaws.

**Utility Pliers.** Utility pliers have wide capacities and can be adjusted to a number of different positions by means of multiposition slip-joints or tongue-and-groove adjustment. They come with handles in various lengths. The longer handles provide greater leverage for gripping and holding objects.

**Long-Nose Pliers.** Long-nose pliers come in a variety of configurations. Designs with and without side cutters are available. Long-nose pliers are used for holding and moving small objects and doing a variety of other intricate tasks frequently required in kite construction. You will probably want to have several shapes and sizes in your tool collection.

**Side-Cutting Pliers.** Side-cutting pliers are useful for holding, bending, and cutting thin materials. They are available in various lengths. The small sizes are especially useful for kite work.

**Locking Pliers.** Locking pliers can be clamped on an object, and they will stay in place. They are available in various sizes. Follow the manufacturer's instructions for adjusting the particular brand.

**Diagonal-Cutting Pliers.** Diagonal-cutting pliers come in various sizes and designs for light and heavy-duty cutting. They are for cutting only and should not be used for gripping and holding objects. Diagonal-cutting pliers are extremely useful in kite construction work for cutting wires, small nails, and so on.

**End-Cutting Pliers.** End-cutting pliers, often called *nippers*, are available in various designs and sizes. They have a good mechanical advantage. Small sizes are generally most useful for kite construction work.

## Clamps

A variety of useful clamps are available to hold parts together for gluing and other tasks. A common and extremely useful type is the C clamp. They come in a variety of sizes; small, light-duty clamps are the most useful for kite construction work. You will probably want to have a number of them in your tool collection.

Paper clips and even clothespins can come in handy for holding small parts together while gluing. Other types of clamps, especially small clamps designed for model building, also will be handy.

## Hammers

Many types and sizes of hammers are available and each is intended for a specific range of uses. Using them for other purposes can damage the hammers or the materials you are working on and may present safety hazards.

**Claw Hammers.** Claw hammers are frequently called *nail* or *carpenter's hammers*. Their purpose is to drive and pull out nails. They are available with either straight or curved claws. The nail-driving face of the hammer might be flat, slightly rounded, or even convex. The plain, flat face is recommended for general-purpose hammering. Some hammers have a wooden handle attached to a steel head; others have a one-piece steel handle and head and a rubber or plastic grip. Fiberglass handles are used on some manufactured hammers. Although claw hammers come in a variety of weights, a lightweight model is generally most useful for kite construction work.

**Ball Peen Hammers.** Ball peen hammers are available with wood, steel, and fiberglass handles. The ball peen end can be used for striking in areas where the face will not fit. They are designed for striking punches and cold chisels, shaping and straightening metal, and riveting work. They come in a variety of weights; lightweight models are the most useful for kite construction.

**Mallets.** Mallets are hammers with soft materials for heads. They are used in situations where a steel hammer would cause damage, as when striking wood and plastic objects. The faces of mallets are made from a variety of materials, including wood, plastic, rawhide, and rubber.

**Tack Hammers.** Tack hammers are designed especially for driving tacks. They are sometimes useful for kite construction work.

## Hole-Making Tools

A portable electric drill will make most hand braces and drills unnecessary for kite construction work. Tools for making holes by hand are useful at times, however, and some people make considerable use of them.

**Twist and Push Drills.** *Twist drills*, which have a hand crank and either a handle or a breast plate, and *push drills*, which rotate when pushed downward, can be used for drilling holes in wood, plastic, and, to a certain extent, metals. They can be useful in situations where an electric drill or electricity is not available. Small models of these drills intended for hobby and craft work are useful for kite construction work.

**Portable Electric Drills.** Many jobs call for making small holes in wood, metal, plastic, and other materials. A ¼-inch drill with about 2,000 r.p.m. is satisfactory for most kite construction. Some drills have a single constant speed; on others the speed is variable and can be adjusted. Some drills allow you to reverse the turning direction.

Cordless electric drills are also available. They have a battery pack located in the handle or in a separate case. Rechargable nickel-cadmium batteries often are used. These drills are useful when you are working without a source of electric power.

Regardless of the type of portable electric drill you use, you will need a selection of standard bits for wood and metal. Small sizes are especially useful. Grinding and sanding attachments also can be used with portable electric drills.

**Drill Presses.** A drill press, which allows more accurate drilling than a hand-held power drill, is useful for advanced kite construction. Many types and sizes are available. Small drill presses allow you to use standard, hand-held, portable electric drills. Small drill presses designed especially for model building are ideal for kite construction work. A variety of attachments for drill presses that make carving, shaping, sanding, and a variety of other jobs possible are also available.

## Screwdrivers

The screwdriver is a basic tool designed for driving and removing screws. A screwdriver also can make a handy pry bar for removing lids from paint cans. Since such jobs tend to ruin good screwdrivers by rounding the corners of the tips and distorting their shapes, only screwdrivers no longer suitable for driving and removing screws should be used as pry bars.

Most screws have an ordinary slotted head. Screws are made in gauge sizes, and each size has a specific slot width and depth. Screwdrivers come with tips designed to fit specific screw-gauge sizes. Ideally, a different size screwdriver is used for each screw gauge, but it is usually possible to use a screwdriver for a screw that is one gauge smaller or larger than that for which the screwdriver was designed.

Small screwdrivers are generally most suitable for kite construction work. Even if you don't use screws as fasteners for kite constructions, you probably will find them useful for adjusting and repairing tools and related uses.

A standard screwdriver for slotted heads should have a straight end on the tip. If the corners are rounded, even slightly, the tip will slip out of the screw slot.

There are also screwdrivers designed for screws with recessed heads. While there are a variety of screwheads of this type in use, the *Phillips head* with a cross slot is the most common. As with standard screwdrivers, always use a Phillips screwdriver that is the correct size for the screw. Small sizes are generally all that will be required for kite construction work.

Regardless of the type, screwdrivers come in various lengths. Greater leverage can be applied to a screw with a long screwdriver.

Handles should feel comfortable and provide a good grip. Handles are often fluted for this purpose. Plastic, wood, and metal handles are all satisfactory.

The price variation in screwdrivers is to a great extent a result of the quality and treatment of the steel used for the shank. The shank must withstand considerable twisting force and must not crumble or break.

Combination screwdrivers with interchangeable blades are also available. They allow a variety of blades to be used with a single handle.

Screwdrivers are also available with springjaw screw holders. They allow one-handed action for starting screws in tight or awkward places. The screws are generally started into pilot holes in this manner and then tightened down with a regular screwdriver. Magnetized screwdrivers that will hold screws for starting are also available. They will only work on magnetic metals, however.

## Planes, Drawknives, and Spokeshaves

Planes, drawknives, and spokeshaves, especially in small sizes designed especially for hobby and craft work, are useful tools for kite construction work. A small plane, for example, can be used to plane and smooth the edges of kite spars. Drawknives and spokeshaves can be used to round the corners of kite spars.

## Files, Rasps, and Surfacing Tools

Files, rasps, and surfacing tools are frequently used in kite-construction work. Files have teeth that are formed by long grooves set at an angle across the faces of the tools. There is a *tang* at one end that fits into the handle, which is usually made of wood or plastic. Files come in a variety of shapes, including rectangular, square, triangular, half-round, and round. Files are made with various degrees of coarseness, which is determined by the number of teeth per square inch of scraping surface. The more teeth per square inch, the smoother the scraping surface. Files are available in various lengths. The smaller sizes are most suitable for typical kite-construction work. You probably also will want a selection of shapes.

Metal files are also useful for kite construction work. Like wood files, they are available in many shapes and sizes. One each of a flat rectangular, square, triangular, and round file will serve to get you started. You can add other shapes and sizes as a need develops. Special brushes and file cards are available for removing the metal filings that tend to clog the file teeth when you use them. Metal files also can be used for filing hard plastic materials.

Rasps have individual teeth that are arranged in staggered rows. They are generally used for rougher work than are files. Like files, rasps have a tang at one end that fits into a handle of wood or plastic. Rasps come in a variety of shapes, including rectangular, square, triangular, half-round, and round. They are made with various degrees of coarseness. For example, for rough shaping of soft woods, a medium-cut rasp with 36 teeth per square inch can be used. For rough shaping of hard woods, a coarse-cut rasp with 26 teeth per square inch might be used. A smooth-cut rasp with 60 teeth per square inch can be used for finishing work.

For each kite-construction job, you will need to select a rasp that has both the desired shape and required coarseness to accomplish the task. Rasps come in various lengths and sizes. The shorter lengths and smaller sizes generally are the most suitable for kite-construction work.

Surfacing tools, also called *forming tools*, are essentially modern versions of traditional rasps. They have improved scraping and cutting action because the blades on the teeth and holes are cut all the way through the blades, thus allowing waste wood or plastic to pass through. Surfacing tools are available in a variety of shapes and sizes, including file types and plane types.

Surfacing tools are ideal for shaping wood and soft and hard plastic materials. Considerable wood can be taken off quickly with them. Their cutting action is generally superior to that of traditional files and rasps. Surfacing tools are also ideal for shaping soft, rigid plastic foam materials, such as Styrofoam, which is used in the construction of many modern kites. Surfacing tools also can be used on hard plastics such as fiberglass. They are available with both flat and rounded blades in a variety of sizes.

Surfacing tools are easy to use. The small sizes and shapes designed for modeling and craft work are especially useful.

## Abrasive Papers and Sanding Tools

Abrasive papers are strong papers that have abrasive materials glued to them. They are frequently called *sandpaper*, although materials other than sand are most commonly used as the abrasive on the papers.

Abrasive papers are graded—the larger the number, the finer the grit. Most sanding starts with coarser grits (smaller grade numbers) and gradually works down to finer grits (larger grade numbers). Selection of abrasive papers will depend on the material to be sanded and the particular job at hand. In addition to any grade or grit numbers, most sandpaper is now sold with designations of coarse, medium-coarse, medium, medium-fine, fine, or very fine. These designations help to avoid confusion when you are purchasing abrasive papers.

The common abrasives used for making abrasive papers include *flint*, which is made of soft sandstone; *garnet*, which is a hard, reddish-brown mineral; and *aluminum oxide* and *silicon carbide*, which are man-made materials. As a general rule, flint abrasive paper is the least expensive, but it does not last long. Garnet and aluminum oxide papers are more expensive, but they last longer and therefore are often the most economical. Silicon carbide is usually the most expensive, but works best for sanding hard abrasive materials, such as fiberglass.

Abrasive papers are sold in both small and large sheets. Large sheets can be cut or torn into smaller pieces that are the right size for hand or block sanding. Abrasive papers can be purchased in packages of assorted grades or grits. Such packages often contain the grades or grits that will be useful for kite-construction work.

You can hold sandpaper by hand or use a sanding block. The choice depends on the job at hand. For maintaining a flat surface, a sanding block is generally recommended. Either a small block of wood or a manufactured sanding block that has provisions for clamping the paper to the block can be used. Small sanding blocks designed for modeling work are especially handy for kite-construction.

Small power sanders designed especially for model work also can be useful for kite-construction work. There are three basic types: a pad sander, a disk sander, and a belt sander.

*Pad sanders* are made with orbital, straight line, and combination orbital and straight line actions. They are designed for finishing and light-duty work. In kite construction work, they can be used for smoothing spars and other similar jobs.

*Disk sanders* have abrasive paper mounted to a rotary disk. They can be attached to hobby rotary tools and portable electric drills. Disk sanders are also available with direct attachment to motors, such as those that attach to scroll saw motors, and with flexible shaft attachments. Disk sanders designed especially for modeling work can be used for kite building.

*Belt sanders,* which have a belt of abrasive paper traveling over two drums, are generally not suitable for most kite construction work. While power sanders can be helpful, they are not essential for making most types of small kites.

## Measuring and Marking Tools

Tools for measuring and marking accurately are important for quality kite construction work. Two measuring systems are still in use: American standard and the metric system. One system can be converted to the other (for example, 1 inch equals 2.540 centimeters), but doing so can be confusing. If you are only familiar with one system, you will probably want to work mainly with it and have your measuring tools in that system. The American standard system is used in this book. A conversion chart or wheel, or a calculator, can be used to convert from one system to the other.

Many types and sizes of rules and tapes are available. For kite construction work, I suggest at least a 1-foot ruler and a yardstick. Steel rulers and straightedges are useful cutting guides for razor blades and knives. A zigzag folding rule or a metal tape rule is useful for measuring longer lengths.

Squares, such as *try squares*, are useful for laying out lines on the materials you are working with. Right-angle triangles, such as those used for drawing and drafting work, can be used similarly.

A variety of drawing and drafting tools, such as drawing boards or tables, T-squares, triangles, protractors, compasses, French curves, and templates, can be useful for laying out patterns on paper and other materials.

A number of devices can be used for marking, including pencils, awls and scribers, pens, crayons, and chalk. The choice depends on the material you are marking. Pencils can be used to mark patterns on wood, paper, and a variety of other materials.

## Vises

At least one vise is almost essential for kite-construction work. To try to get along without one can greatly reduce the quality of the work. A small vise of either the clamp-on variety or the bench-mounted type can be used. These vises are generally considered to be metal-working vises, but you can clamp all kinds of materials in them.

You don't need a very big vise for constructing small kites, but I suggest a quality vise. The small models designed for modeling and craft work are ideal, although larger vises also can be used.

A woodworking bench vise or a work stand with a built-in vise, especially a small hobby unit, also can be useful for kite-construction work. The work stands are discussed later in this chapter.

## Rotary Hobby Tools

Miniature rotary grinding tools, such as those made by Dremel, Foredom, and Casco, can be useful for some kite-construction jobs. These tools have attachments for grinding, drilling, carving, brushing, cutting, sanding, and a variety of other jobs. Rotary hobby tools rate high with many kite builders. A single tool with appropriate attachments can do a variety of jobs that are typically encountered in kite construction.

Rotary tool attachments also can be used on a flexible shaft that attaches to a fixed motor. Dremel, for example, makes a flexible shaft attachment that connects to the company's scroll saws. They can be used in a manner similar to the portable hand tools.

## Soldering Tools

Soldering can add new dimensions to kite building. Soldering irons can be used for joining a variety of metals to make fittings for kites. They also can be used to seal and join a variety of synthetic fabrics.

There are two basic types of soldering irons: pencil and gun. The pencil types generally take some time to heat up, but they provide a constant heat after that. The gun type heat up almost at once. Both types can be used for kite-construction work; however, I find the pencil type to be more useful.

Regardless of the tool you use for providing heat, you will need solder and resin or acid to join metals together. Solders come in various mixtures of tin and lead or other metals. The choice depends on the particular metals you intend to join. Solder is available with the resin or acid as a core material, or you can purchase solder without a core, purchase the required resin or acid separately, and apply it to the metal with a brush applicator. Solder is generally sold with directions for using it, what metals can be joined with it, and so on.

It will take some practice to learn to solder but it can be worthwhile to learn, especially for advanced kite-construction work.

## Other Tools

The tools discussed so far are the most important ones for kite-construction work, but there are many other tools that you may find useful.

A round-hole paper punch is handy for making neat holes to pass strings through paper kites. Paper punches can be purchased wherever stationery and office supplies are sold.

Tweezers are useful for handling small parts and pulling string through loops and other tight places.

Although a rotary hobby tool can be used for grinding and wire brushing operations, I find a larger bench-mounted power grinder is also useful, especially for sharpening tools used for kite-construction work. I like a grinding wheel on one end and a wire brush on the other. The wire brush is useful for cleaning metal parts.

You also will need brushes and various other tools for painting and decorating kites (see Chapter 3).

Wrenches are frequently required for adjusting and repairing tools. Wrenches are available in a variety of types, including box, end, and adjustable configurations. If you intend to use small bolts as fasteners on kites, you will need small wrenches that fit them.

As you go along in kite construction, you probably will find that you need other tools. They can be added to your tool collection when a need develops. Kite construction tool collections have a way of growing as your interest and involvement in this hobby increase.

## SAFETY EQUIPMENT

Compared to many construction hobbies, kite construction is reasonably safe. You will, however, be working with tools that have sharp blades, paints and glues that might have toxic fumes or vapors, and so on. You will need all safety guards and other equipment required for the safe use of power tools.

For grinding and sanding, especially with power tools, you will need safety goggles made of tough plastic materials. Many models will fit over eyeglasses. They are quite inexpensive compared to the degree of protection they provide.

You also will need a disposable dust mask. These should not be used for toxic vapors or fumes, however. For this purpose, you will need a respirator designed especially to provide protection from the particular vapors or fumes. A plastic face shield can be worn whenever you are doing grinding work.

## WORKBENCHES

It is often said that you can use the kitchen table as a workbench for a hobby like constructing kites. Well, perhaps, but there are a number of problems with doing so. First, kitchen tables are generally not sturdy enough to be considered "real" workbenches. Second, you can easily damage the kitchen table, especially if you use a saw or power tools. Third, you usually will have to share the table with other things (like eating). Also, kitchen tables usually are not appropriately located for kite-construction work. If you do sanding, for example, will the sawdust you generate get mixed in with food?

It is much better to have a "real" workbench for kite-construction work. If you already have a workbench that you have been using for general woodworking, modeling work, or other uses, you probably also can use it for your kite-construction work. It is generally much better to share a workbench than to share a kitchen table.

You also can purchase or build workbenches to suit your particular needs. Here are some important considerations:

❖ A workbench should be sturdy. If you already have a workbench that is not sturdy enough, add braces or reinforcements to improve it.

❖ A workbench should be at a convenient working height, either for sitting or standing, depending on how you like to work.

❖ A workbench should have a top of adequate size for the work you intend to do. For general kite-construction work, a top that is 2 feet by 3 feet is about the minimum practical size. A larger working area is usually better.

❖ Space and storage areas for tools, materials, and supplies are important considerations.

A small portable shop bench is a useful addition to a permanent workbench, but not a substitute for it. The unit shown has a built-in vise and clamping arrangement that is extremely useful. The model shown has its own stand, but others are available for use on workbenches. They are especially designed for hobby and craft work.

## WORK AREAS

A work area should provide protection from the weather (although it can be outdoors if the weather is good), yet allow you to do jobs such as sanding, painting, and sawing. Garages, basements, and hobby or recreation rooms typically are suitable locations. Here are some important considerations:

❖ The area should allow for messy work, such as sanding, sawing, and painting. Rooms in your house that contain rugs and furniture generally aren't suitable.

❖ The area should have good ventilation. If you plan to do much painting, you might want to consider adding an exhaust fan.

❖ Good lighting is important. It is difficult to do quality kite-construction work if you can't see what you are doing. The lighting can be natural, artificial, or a combination of both.

❖ The area should be used exclusively for kite construction or shared with other compatible activities.

## MATERIALS

A variety of materials, from traditional wood, bamboo, paper, and cotton string to modern synthetics, are used in modern kite construction.

## Wood

Regardless of whether you use softwood or hardwood, you will need sticks of the desired size. You can cut your own from larger stock, or you can purchase sticks precut to various sizes. Dowels, which come in various diameters, are readily available and suitable for many kite constructions. Square and other rectangular shapes in small sizes suitable for kite sticks are also readily available.

Wood, along with bamboo, is a traditional material for making kite sticks. As a general rule, you will want to use the lightest and strongest woods available, but because the heavier woods are also frequently the strongest woods, compromises will need to be made. The best compromises to make will depend on the particular kite you are making.

Both softwoods (coniferous trees) and hardwoods (deciduous trees) can be used as kite sticks and framing. The choice depends on the particular kite being constructed. For some kites, the extra strength of the hardwoods would not compensate for the extra weight; for other types and/or sizes of kites, it would.

**Balsa Wood.** Balsa wood is a lightweight wood. Balsa is a fast-growing tree of tropical America. Most balsa wood comes from Ecuador. Balsa is botanically a hardwood, but physically it is very soft, in fact, one of the softest and lightest of all commercial woods. The approximate weight per cubic foot of air-seasoned balsa is 8 pounds. The heartwood is usually pale brown, sometimes slightly tinged with red. The sapwood varies from white to pale gray, and it has a uniform texture.

While balsa wood is widely used in making models, it has only limited usefulness as kite sticks because it lacks strength. When used as kite sticks, it tends to snap from stresses placed on the kite by the wind and other factors. Balsa wood is often adequate, however, for miniature kites.

Balsa wood is readily available from hobby stores precut to sticks of various dimensions. This is a very convenient way to purchase balsa for kite construction. You also can purchase balsa in larger dimensions and use a ripsaw to cut it into the desired stick sizes.

If you want to cut balsa with a knife, a razor-type blade is usually required. A razor blade also can be used.

Sheets of balsa, available from hobby stores, are sometimes used as covering material for miniature and small kites.

**White Pine.** White pine is grown in the United States from Maine to northern Georgia and in lake states. The botanical classification is softwood. The approximate weight per cubic foot of air-seasoned white pine is 25 pounds. It is a finely textured wood with a yellow-white color and is an excellent wood for sticks on many types and sizes of kites. It is an easy wood with which to work, is fairly inexpensive, and is widely available in the United States. Of all the domestic pine woods, white pine is probably the most suitable for use as kite sticks.

**Ponderosa Pine.** Ponderosa pine grows in California, Oregon, Washington, Idaho, Montana, the southern Rockies, South Dakota, and Wyoming. It is considered to be the most important pine tree of the western United States. The botanical classification is softwood. The approximate weight per cubic foot of air-seasoned ponderosa pine is 28 pounds. The color of the wood is a light yellowish white. Ponderosa pine has a straight and uniform grain, which makes it ideal for kite sticks. It is also an easy wood with which to work, is readily available, and is fairly inexpensive.

**Sugar Pine.** Sugar pine grows in California and southwestern Oregon. The botanical classification is softwood. The approximate weight per cubic foot of air-seasoned sugar pine is 25 pounds. It has a straight and uniform grain, making it ideal for kite sticks. It is also an easy wood with which to work, is readily available, and is fairly inexpensive.

**Spruce.** Spruce is a name applied to any of the various coniferous evergreen trees of the genus *Picea*. The three main kinds are eastern spruce, Engelmann spruce, and Sitka spruce. All are lightweight woods that are botanically classified as softwoods. The approximate weight per cubic foot of air-seasoned spruce is 28 pounds.

Spruce, especially Sitka spruce, has long been a favorite wood for kite sticks. It is a strong wood that is easily worked. It is readily available and reasonably priced, although generally more expensive than pine woods.

**Douglas Fir.** Douglas fir grows from the Pacific Coast to the Rockies, and from central British Columbia to Mexico. It is botanically a softwood. The approximate weight per cubic foot of air-seasoned Douglas fir is 31 pounds. The color varies from pale to medium red-brown. It is a moderately dense wood with a straight, close grain and is one of the strongest of the botanical softwoods. Douglas fir is suitable for kite sticks, although it does have considerable tendency to split and check. Douglas fir is readily available and fairly inexpensive.

Other fir woods, including Western fir and white fir, also can be used for making kite spars.

**Other Softwoods.** There are hundreds of other softwoods that can and have been successfully used for making kite sticks and frames. In many cases, you will be able to use whatever softwoods you happen to have on hand or can obtain in the area you live. Keep in mind, however, that some will work better than others.

**Hardwoods.** For some kites, hardwoods can be used for the sticks. One popular choice is ash. Ash grows in many parts of the United States, and is often readily available and inexpensive. The approximate weight per cubic foot of air-seasoned ash is 45 pounds. It is a heavy, hard, and strong wood with a straight grain.

Another popular hardwood is oak. Oak grows in North America, Europe, and northern Asia. The approximate weight per cubic foot of air-seasoned oak is 43 pounds. Oak is a hard, strong wood with great lasting qualities.

The two types most readily available in the United States are red oak and white oak. Oak is generally fairly expensive.

Many other hardwoods also can be used for making kite sticks. You might want to do some experimenting with locally available types.

## Bamboo

Bamboo is another traditional material for making kite sticks, especially in China and Japan. Bamboo also is used extensively for modern kites and is readily available in the United States. One possibility is to cut lengths of bamboo pole (the stems of bamboo) into narrow strips for kite sticks. Another possibility is to purchase the bamboo already cut into narrow strips. (A bamboo window shade can provide a quantity of suitable strips of bamboo.)

## Other Materials

There is a strong trend toward using various plastics for kite sticks. A variety of rigid plastic rods and tubings give the necessary combination of light weight and strength. Fiberglass rod, for example, is extremely strong, yet flexible. While the fabrication of fiberglass kite sticks from resin and glass fibers is quite involved, prefabricated fiberglass rods can be purchased. One excellent source is old fiberglass fishing rods, which turn up frequently at flea markets and junk stores.

Various lightweight metal alloys, such as aluminum, also can be used for kite sticks. For large kites, this choice becomes quite practical.

## Covering Materials

A variety of materials can be used for covering kites. Paper is the most traditional material, and it remains a popular choice today. Many kinds of paper can be used, including newspapers, tissue paper, craft paper, and rice paper. Strong, lightweight papers that do not permit air to pass through them are ideal.

Cloth materials are becoming increasingly popular for use as kite-covering materials. Silk has long been popular, and ordinary muslin is sometimes used for larger kites. Lightweight nylon is suitable for even small kites. It is available in weights of 1 ounce or less per square yard. Various nylon materials fabricated for sailboat spinnakers make an excellent kite-covering material.

Various plastic materials are rapidly replacing paper as the favorite kite-covering material. Polyethylene plastic, which is the type that many garbage and garment bags are made from, is a popular choice. It is readily obtainable. Polyethylene sheet plastic is available in various thicknesses and colors.

Various other plastic materials, such as Mylar, are increasingly popular for use as kite-covering materials. Mylar is strong and lightweight. It is quite expensive, but is often worth the price when you need a covering material that is extremely lightweight and strong.

The choice of a covering material for a particular kite depends on the particular design, the size of the kite, and other factors. For some of the designs detailed in this book, a variety of covering materials will give satisfactory results. In other cases, a certain type of covering material will be essential. Also, you may want to experiment with new materials as they come on the market.

## String and Thread

String or line is used not only for flying kites, but also for framing kites, binding sticks and frame pieces together, and making bridles. String and line made from natural materials is rapidly being replaced by synthetic materials. Polyester and twisted nylon string are both popular. Polyester has the advantage of having less stretch and being easier to tie. Nylon monofilament line, such as the type sold as fishing line, is another possibility, although it can be difficult to tie.

Thread can be used as string for small kites. Even small-gauge polyester and nylon thread can have a high breaking strength. Thread can be used like string for binding kite sticks together, and it is also useful for sewing covering fabrics.

## Glues

A variety of modern glues are ideal for general kite construction. White hobby glues can be used for joining a variety of porous materials, including heavier grades of paper. Rubber and various plastic cements can be used for lighter papers. A variety of plastic cements formulated for model building are ideal for many kite construction jobs. Epoxy glues are ideal for making strong wood joints. Quick-drying epoxy glues that are sold for hobby use give excellent results. Plastic materials require special glues, as detailed later in this chapter.

## Other Materials

There are many other materials useful for kite constructions. A variety of tapes including cellulose adhesive tape, strapping tape, and plastic tape can be used for joining materials, reinforcement, or decoration.

Fasteners can be used for joining kite parts—pins, small wire brads and nails, screws, and bolts.

Small wire is useful for a variety of jobs. A variety of metals and plastics can be used for making kite fittings. For example, a section of plastic tubing can be used to join two wooden dowels that will just fit inside the tubing. Thin sheets of aluminum, brass, and copper are useful for fabricating small metal fittings.

Rigid plastic foam materials, especially Styrofoam, are being used increasingly for kite construction. Thin sheets can be used as a covering material on some kites. Kites also can be formed from sheets of Styrofoam without the use of kite sticks. In this case, the Styrofoam acts as both the frame and the covering material.

For decorating kites, you may need paints, dyes, and other materials, as detailed in Chapter 3.

# BASIC CONSTRUCTION TECHNIQUES

This section is extremely important. Once you master the basic skills and techniques of kite making, the construction of a variety of interesting kites will be relatively easy. You can use these same techniques for constructing original kite designs.

One good source of kite supplies is Into the Wind, 2047 Broadway, Boulder, CO 80302. Telephone: (303) 449-5356.

## Kite Sticks and Frames

A kite's frame members are often called *sticks* or *spars*. We will use the term *stick* to refer to long, slender frame members, regardless of whether they are wood, bamboo, metal, plastic, or some other material.

An important part of many kite constructions is assembling the individual sticks into frames. Various methods are used for joining sticks. Many frames also require various reinforcements.

**Wood Frames.** A variety of woods can be used for kite sticks. Kite sticks can be one of a variety of cross-sectional shapes, including square, rectangular, triangular, and round. You can purchase sticks preshaped in a variety of woods. You also can cut square and rectangular shapes from larger wood stock using a variety of saws. To make accurate and straight cuts, use a circular table power saw with a guide. You also can use hand saws, but straight and accurate cutting can be difficult. A knife can be used to cut balsa and other soft woods into strips. You can use a knife and either a metal straightedge as a guide or a special knife guide designed for this purpose.

After cutting the wood into sticks with the correct cross sections, you will need to do sanding to smooth the edges. Use a sanding block to maintain an even surface.

Next cut the sticks to the required lengths for a particular kite construction. Mark the pattern lines for the cuts on the wood with a sharp pencil. For accurate square cuts, use a square to make the pattern line. You can use a knife to cut balsa and other soft woods, or a saw for both softwoods and hardwoods. Fasten the wood in a vise for sawing.

For many kites, the sticks will require notches in the ends for string or connections to other sticks. Mark the pattern lines on the wood with a sharp pencil. You can cut these lines in balsa and softwoods with a knife, or you can use a coping saw, power jigsaw, or scroll saw for both softwoods and hardwoods.

**Bamboo.** Bamboo makes an excellent framing material for kites and was probably used for the first kites. You can purchase bamboo precut into narrow strips or slats, or you can take them from the roll-up type of bamboo shades. You also can cut your own strips from bamboo poles.

To cut a bamboo pole into sticks, first cut the pole into a length slightly longer than the longest stick that you will need. You can use a hacksaw to cut the bamboo.

Next, split the pole in half using a knife with a sharp blade. Take half of the bamboo and use a knife with a sharp blade to split it into strips of the desired width, using the same technique used to halve the pole. Repeat the same procedure on the other half of the pole.

Next use a sharp knife to smooth the bamboo strips and shape them as desired. The knuckles should be trimmed slightly. This procedure must be done carefully, however. The basic idea is to make the stick as neat as possible without creating a weak area at the knuckle.

In some cases, further shaping will be required. The sticks might require taper near the ends or even a variety of thicknesses in the same stick. Most kite constructions, however, require basically straight sticks of uniform thicknesses along the entire length. Regardless of the cross section of the sticks, you can sand them smooth using a sanding block. In some cases, the sticks are rounded. To round a stick, first use a sharp knife to round off the corners. Then even up the cuts and sand smooth with a sanding block.

Many kite constructions require notches in the ends of the sticks. You can use a coping saw or power jig or scroll saw for this operation. Mark the pattern line on the bamboo, then fasten the bamboo in a vise to saw.

You easily can form bamboo to desired curves by heating it. First, mark the desired curve on a piece of cardboard. Then move the bamboo through a candle flame and bend it to the desired curve, using the pattern on the cardboard as a guide. When heating bamboo, take care not to hold the bamboo in one position too long, or you might deform the bamboo or even burn it. Overheating bamboo tends to make it brittle.

For most kite constructions, the bamboo is underbent so that it will have spring tension. For example, to form a circle, the circle is underbent. When the ends of the bamboo are joined together, the circle will be under spring tension, resulting in a stronger frame. Small sticks sometimes can be formed into circles without heating. You then can use heating to remove any irregularities in the circle.

In some cases, you can use small-diameter bamboo poles for kite sticks, without cutting them into strips. The result is a round stick with considerable strength. Bamboo poles can be heat-formed in the same manner as strips.

**Rattan.** Rattan also is used for making curved or bowed kite sticks. Diameters of from about ⅛ inch to ¼ inch in diameter are useful. Rattan can be heat-formed in the same manner as bamboo.

**Metal.** Lightweight metals and alloys, especially thin-walled aluminum tubing, are being used increasingly for kite sticks. Aluminum rods and tubing are available in various sizes and lengths from hobby shops and hardware stores. Aluminum is also available in various other cross-sectional shapes, including square, rectangular, triangular, I beam, and L shape.

All cross sections of aluminum can be cut with a hacksaw or other metal-cutting saw. You can use a tube cutter to cut aluminum tubing.

Aluminum can be bent to form curved kite sticks. Aluminum rod and square and rectangular cross sections can be bent by hand or over various forms, such as around a metal drum for a circle shape. Aluminum tubing can be bent similarly, except that there is considerable danger of deforming the walls of the tubing. This danger can be largely avoided by using a tube bender. Inexpensive tube benders are available for small-diameter tubing at hobby and hardware stores.

Other metals and alloys also can be used for kite spars, especially those that are very light in weight.

**Plastic.** A great variety of plastic materials are available for kite sticks, and these have different properties that affect cutting, filing, sanding, and working. The properties of plastic materials that can be used for kite sticks and frames vary greatly, but many can be cut with hacksaws or other metal-cutting saws. Many can be filed with metal files. It will take some experimentation to determine what tools and techniques work best for a particular plastic. Some plastics in hardened form can be heat-formed; others can't. Some plastics are available in preshaped forms, such as rings, that are suitable for certain kite constructions. Plastic ring frames also can be cut from plastic bottles and other plastic objects.

A variety of plastic rods and tubes, as well as other cross-sectional shapes, have the necessary combination of strength, rigidity, and light weight for use as kite frames and sticks. Flexible and semirigid plastics show much promise for kites that require semirigid forms.

Fiberglass rod increasingly is being used as a kite-framing material. Compared to its weight, fiberglass is a strong, flexible, and resilient material. Fiberglass is a combination of glass fiber reinforcing material and a resin, usually polyester or epoxy, that is used to form a hard composite material having great strength. The physical properties of fiberglass depend on the type and amount of glass fiber reinforcing material, the type and quality of resin, the fabrication method, and other factors.

Fiberglass is available in preshaped rod forms of various diameters that are suitable for making kite frames. Old fiberglass fishing rods, which are often available from junk and thrift stores, are another possibility.

Various nonglass reinforcing materials, including acrylic and carbon fibers, are being used with plastic resins to form fiberglasslike materials. Carbon fiber reinforced plastic forms a material that has a greater strength-to-weight ratio than does fiberglass. This material, while very expensive, shows great promise for making lightweight kites that are extremely strong.

Fiberglass has considerable potential for use as kite sticks and frames. We will assume that you will be using preshaped fiberglass rods or other preshaped lengths of fiberglass to make kite sticks and frames. *Fiberglassing* (chemically forming fiberglass from liquid resin and fiberglass reinforcing materials) will be considered later in this chapter only for the purpose of bonding fiberglass sticks and frames together. You could, however, make your own sticks and frame pieces from liquid resin and reinforcing materials, thus allowing you to vary thicknesses for strength where it is required while keeping weight to an absolute minimum.

When you are working with cured fiberglass, you should observe certain health and safety precautions. Anyone who has sanded fiberglass without skin protection knows that fiberglass sanding dust makes your skin itch. This fine dust also is raised when cured fiberglass is sawed, filed, and ground. This dust also can cause eye and respiratory problems.

You can wear protective clothing to keep the fiberglass dust from your skin. If, despite all precautions, some sanding dust does get on the skin, a cold shower followed by application of hand lotion often will help to relieve itching. If skin rash or other unusual reactions develop, consult a physician.

A properly fitted dust mask and eye goggles will give respiratory and eye protection. These precautions are extremely important.

Wearing proper protective clothing for working with cured fiberglass might be uncomfortable, especially in hot weather, but this slight discomfort and inconvenience is a necessary and important sacrifice for the protection of your health.

Frequent operations that will be required on cured fiberglass members include drilling, sawing, filing, and sanding. It is generally easy to drill small holes in fiberglass. Although you can use a hand drill, a portable electric drill or drill press will make the work much easier. Metal twist bits can be used, but you must have a different size for each hole size you intend to drill. Before drilling, carefully mark the desired location for the hole. Use a center punch or other sharp-pointed object to make a small indentation, or *pilot mark*, for centering the point of the bit. Center the point of the bit in a small indentation. Angle the drill as desired and drill the hole through the fiberglass.

There are many situations where you will want to saw fiberglass. For example, fiberglass rods for kite sticks probably will require cutting. You can do the cutting with a hacksaw or a coping saw with a fine-toothed cutting blade. When you are making critical cuts, leave a little extra and then use a file to take it to final size.

You can cut notches in the ends of fiberglass frame pieces with a hacksaw or a coping saw with a fine-toothed cutting blade.

You can use metal files for filing fiberglass to round the ends of frame pieces, and to shape and make grooves and notches. As a general rule, pressure is applied to the file on the forward stroke only. Lift the file off the work when you are drawing it back. If the file notches become clogged with fiberglass, use a file brush or solvent to clean them.

You also can use a variety of small surfacing tools for shaping fiberglass. They are used similarly to files.

You can sand fiberglass with aluminum oxide or silicon carbide sandpaper. The general principle in sanding fiberglass is to start with the coarsest grit required for the particular job and then progressively work down to finer grits. You can hold the sandpaper by hand, or you can use a sanding block. Hold the sandpaper in place around the block while you sand. You also can use special blocks or flexible holders that have a clamping arrangement for holding the paper in place. Block sanding allows the removal of high spots without affecting adjacent low areas.

You also can use sanding and grinding attachments in rotary hobby tools for power sanding and grinding fiberglass.

## Joining Sticks and Frame Members

Kite sticks and frame members frequently are joined by binding or lashing them together with string or thread, often in combination with glue. Wooden or bamboo members, especially, are joined in this way. If the joint is also to be glued, first apply glue, as detailed later, then tightly lash the two sticks together and tie with a square knot. Glue also can be applied to the lashings.

An alternative to using thread or string bindings is to use strapping tape or other suitable tape. The joints can be with or without glue, as desired. Strapping tape alone often provides satisfactory joints, especially for small kites.

You can join wooden and bamboo sticks end to end by splicing. These joints often are glued first, then lashed together with string or thread. Tie with a square knot. You also can apply glue to the lashings to further reinforce the joint.

Kite sticks and frame members also can be joined by gluing, either alone or in combination with mechanical fastening. The choice of glue will depend on the materials being joined. In some cases, several types of glue will give satisfactory results. White resin-emulsion glue can be used for joining wood, bamboo, and a variety of other porous materials. Follow the manufacturer's directions for using the particular brand. In many cases, a thin coat of glue is applied to each surface. The joint is then clamped together until the glue has dried.

Epoxy glue gives good results on both porous and nonporous materials. Epoxy *cures* rather than dries. It usually comes in two parts, which must be mixed together before use. Mix only what you need for a particular job. Once the two parts have been mixed together, the mixture will cure even in a sealed container. The newer, quick-drying epoxy glues are especially suitable for kite-construction work.

Epoxy glues do present certain safety hazards if they are improperly handled or used. Follow the manufacturer's directions for the safe use of the particular product. In general, avoid skin contact, and avoid breathing fumes or vapors. Use the glue only in a well-ventilated area. If a skin rash or any other unusual reactions develop, consult a physician.

A variety of acetate cements and plastic cements, such as those formulated for modeling and hobby work, also can be used for joining kite sticks. Follow the manufacturer's directions carefully when you are using these products.

A number of "super" glues that are rapid setting and anaerobic are now on the market. These glues often advertise that a single drop will provide tons of holding power. I haven't had very good results with these glues. Some joints have popped apart when little or no loads were applied, but you might have better results than I have had. As a general rule, the glue is applied to one side of the joint and the parts are pressed together. Be careful when you are using these glues, as they also will glue your fingers together or glue you to whatever you are working on.

Sticks also can be joined with nails, bolts, screws, and other similar mechanical fasteners. Care must be taken, however, so that holes made in the sticks do not form a weak area that is likely to snap when the kite is flown. It is perhaps for this reason that these types of mechanical fasteners are not often used in the construction of small kites.

Various fittings can be used as connecting links for joining parts. A variety of molded plastic fittings are available from hobby supply stores. They provide a convenient way to join round kite stick into a variety of kite frame patterns. If the sticks fit tightly in the fittings or are held by tension, glue might not be be necessary. In some cases, you also will want to glue the sticks into the fittings.

Plastic tubing also can be used to make connections. For example, rigid plastic tubing can be used to join two round sticks end to end. Flexible tubing, such as a clear polyethylene, can be used for a variety of connections.

Aluminum and other lightweight metal and alloy tubing can be used for making a variety of connecting fittings. You also can fabricate a number of useful fittings from thin sheets of aluminum or other metals and alloys.

Kite frame joints are sometimes reinforced with *gussets*, such as triangular wooden inserts and metal angle braces. A variety of lightweight plastic and metal reinforcing members that are suitable for kite construction are available from hobby stores.

Another useful method for joining kite sticks is fiberglassing. A lightweight fiberglass cloth tape (make certain that it is intended for fiberglass lay-up work) is saturated with a rapid-curing epoxy resin (with hardener added) and wrapped around the sticks to be joined.

A typical application involves shaping and cleaning the sticks to be joined, which can be wood, bamboo, rattan, aluminum, fiberglass, or a variety of other materials. First cut the fiberglass cloth tape to suitable sizes. Then mix the epoxy resin with the hardener according to the manufacturer's directions. Place the fiberglass cloth on a piece of cardboard and, using a brush, saturate it with epoxy resin. Then wrap the cloth around the parts to be joined. Apply additional pieces of fiberglass reinforcing material saturated with epoxy resin, as required. Clamp or prop the sticks in position and allow the epoxy resin to cure.

## String Guys and Guidelines

String often is attached to kite sticks for use as guys, guidelines, and for other purposes. A basic two-stick kite, for example, has a string guideline around it that passes through notches in the ends of the sticks. The string serves as a frame for the covering material, and also as guys for bracing the kite sticks and holding them in a cross position. To make a string guy, route the string through the notches in the kite sticks, and join the ends of the string together with a square knot.

Often, you will want to reinforce the notches, especially those of wooden sticks and bamboo sticks, by *string lashings*. First wind the lashing around the stick, usually both above and below the guideline, and then tie it with a square knot.

String guys are frequently used to bow kites. This method also serves to put the bowed kite stick under tension. Usually, you will first wind the string to a notch in one end of the stick and tie it, usually with a square knot. Then bow the stick by hand pressure, wind the guy string, and tie it with the desired tension to a notch on the other end of the stick.

# 3
# Finishing Kites

Once you have made the frame for your kite, you will need to cover it, add a tail, and decorate it. Then you can take it out and watch it fly.

## KITE-COVERING MATERIALS

A variety of covering materials can be used for kites. The choice will depend on the particular kite, availability, and other factors. For some kites, the choice of covering material is crucial; for others you will have a choice of two or more different materials.

Silk was probably the earliest material used for kite coverings, and it is still sometimes used today. Paper also was used as a covering material for early kites. Over the long history of kites, it has been the most widely used covering material. Modern synthetic materials and plastic films are rapidly becoming the most popular kite-covering materials.

An important aspect of kite-covering materials is their attachment to the kite frames and guideline strings. Methods for attaching various materials follow.

## Paper

Paper has a long tradition as a kite-covering material in many parts of the world, and it remains popular today.

A wide range of papers can be used as kite-covering materials. One of the lightest papers is tissue paper. It does tend to tear rather easily, but it has adequate tear strength for many smaller kites.

Newspaper is another possibility. It is readily available, but has a low tear strength in relation to its weight, which tends to limit its usefulness. Many kites have been covered with newspaper and successfully flown, however, and it is likely that this practice will continue.

Many specialty papers, such as rice paper, can be used for covering kites. Art and craft stores often have a variety of lightweight papers that you might want to consider.

Papers suitable for kite-covering materials range in weight from quite light, like tissue paper, up to heavy, such as thin cardboard. Not all papers, however, are suitable for all kites. The choice will depend on the particular kite design, the size of the kite, the way the kite will be decorated, and so on.

Papers can be joined together and to kite frames by a number of adhesives, including white resin-emulsion glue, rubber cement, and a variety of adhesive tapes. Many different techniques can be used for decorating paper, which is one of the reasons for its popularity as a kite-covering material.

Many papers allow little or no air to pass through them. For most kite constructions, it is an advantage to have a covering material that does not allow air to pass through it.

As a general rule, first mark the pattern on the paper. Typically, you will want to use flaps for forming sleeves for guideline strings and for joining ends of paper together. Use scissors to cut the paper to the desired pattern.

In some cases, you will want to paint the paper or otherwise decorate it before gluing or taping it to kite frames or to form sleeves for guideline strings. In other cases, you won't decorate the kite, or you will decorate it after the paper has been installed on the kite frame.

When you are gluing the paper, follow the manufacturer's directions for the particular glue used. In some cases, you will apply the glue to one surface only; in other cases, you will apply the glue to both surfaces. Then press the parts together.

You can reinforce paper in areas of high stress by gluing a piece of paper to the covering material. Adhesive tape can be used similarly. Gummed binder hole rings are handy for reinforcing areas where strings pass through the paper.

## Silk and Cotton

Silk and various cotton fabrics of reasonably dense construction (so that little air will pass through the material) have long been popular kite-covering materials. Silk and suitable cotton fabrics range in weight from light to medium. The materials can be joined by sewing, fabric glue, and various adhesive tapes. Decorating techniques include printing and dyeing. Silk and cotton fabrics usually have from medium to high tear strength, making them suitable for many medium to large kites, but these materials rapidly are being replaced by modern synthetic materials.

To cover a kite with silk or cotton material, first mark the desired pattern on the material with chalk or dressmaker's tracing paper. Use scissors to cut the material to the pattern.

Sleeves can be formed, ends of the material joined together, or two pieces of material joined by hand or machine sewing. If you use a sewing machine, a zigzag stitch usually gives the strongest joints, although straight stitching patterns also can be used.

## Modern Synthetic Fabrics

A variety of lightweight synthetic fabrics of nylon, polyester, and materials such as those designed for sails make excellent kite-covering materials. These materials typically have tear strengths ranging from medium to high. A full range of weights, from light to heavy, are available. The lightest weights are generally the most suitable for kite construction. These materials come in a rainbow of colors and can be joined by sewing or taping. These fabrics generally have low porosity, or even zero porosity, making them ideal for most kite constructions.

First, mark the patterns on the fabric with chalk, transfer paper, or other means. Use scissors to cut the fabric to the pattern.

The material can be sewn by hand or machine, as desired. Polyester thread works well for most synthetic fabrics. If you use a sewing machine, a zigzag stitch will generally give the strongest joint, although straight stitching patterns usually also will give satisfactory results.

## Plastic Films

Plastic films are extremely popular kite covering materials. One reason for their popularity is their wide availability in the form of plastic leaf and trash can bags. A variety of plastic films, including polyethylene and polyurethane, can be used. These films typically have low to medium tear strength and are available in weights from light to heavy. Most are nonporous, making them ideal for covering many types of kites.

Polyethylene, as well as a number of other similar plastic films, can be joined by heat sealing or by adhesive tapes, such as transparent cellulose adhesive tape. Heat-sealing tools, such as those designed for sealing food in plastic bags, are ideal for joining plastic films. Some plastic adhesives also will work, but use a test strip to be certain that it gives a satisfactory bond and does not dissolve the plastic.

Polyethylene and other similar plastic films are too thin to be sewn, although some plastic materials, such as thin vinyl, sometimes can be satisfactorily sewn. If you will use a sewing machine, try it first with a test strip of the plastic. Use a long stitch length to provide more space between needle holes and less chance of the plastic tearing under stress.

Solvent-based marking pens can be used to decorate polyethylene and a number of other similar plastic films.

You can make a typical plastic-film kite cover by first marking the pattern on the plastic. Then cut the plastic to the pattern with scissors. Make plastic joints to form sleeves and join ends, using one of the methods just detailed.

A plastic film that works especially well for kite construction is Mylar, which is a Du Pont product. It has a high tear strength and is available in a range of weights, from extremely light to heavy. The light weights are the most suitable for kite constructions. The extremely high strength-to-weight ratio of this material allows for very lightweight kites. Mylar is available in a variety of colors.

Mylar can be joined by using Mylar tape and other adhesive tapes. Solvent-based marking pens can be used for marking and decorating this material.

Another new material being used for covering kites is Tyvek, also a Du Pont product. Tyvek is a spun-bonded olefin that has an extremely high tear strength in relation to its weight. It can be glued with rubber cement as well as some other glues. If you are uncertain if a particular glue will work, glue a test strip first. The material also can be sewn, and it can be cut with scissors.

Some plastic materials can be joined with small grommets. Special tools are available for punching the holes for these and setting the grommets. Grommets are also useful for reinforcing the areas where bridle, bow, and other strings pass through the material.

## BRIDLE ATTACHMENTS

Bridle strings typically attach to kite sticks, in some cases first passing through holes in the kite-covering material. They also can attach to the kite-covering material, especially on kites that have keels. When bridle strings pass through covering material, the material is frequently reinforced by tape, gummed binder rings, grommets, or other means. Kite sticks sometimes are notched slightly in the area where bridle strings are attached to keep the string from sliding. Square knots often are used to tie the string to the sticks. (Additional information about bridles is included in Chapter 4.)

## KITE TAILS

A variety of tails are used on kites. Plastic and fabric tails are sometimes extensions of the covering material or extension strips that are glued, taped, sewn, or tied to the kite-covering material, the frame, or both. In some cases, the tails have string attachments to the kites.

## OTHER USEFUL SKILLS AND TECHNIQUES

A variety of other skills and techniques are useful for kite construction, including working with Styrofoam and other rigid-plastic foam materials, constructing heads and other forms for use on kites, applying model airplane construction techniques, and using soldering techniques.

### Rigid-Plastic Foam Materials

Styrofoam (polystyrene expanded approximately 40 times) and other lightweight rigid-plastic foam materials are being used increasingly for kite constructions. Styrofoam has the combination of both light and adequate strength and is, therefore, suitable for both the framework and covering material. Styrofoam also can be used as a covering material for some framed kites.

Styrofoam is available at craft and hobby stores in sheet and block form. Pieces of Styrofoam from packing cartons sometimes can also be used, although this material tends to be heavier than the Styrofoam sold in craft and hobby stores.

You can use a sharp knife or razor blade to cut Styrofoam. First, mark the pattern lines on the Styrofoam with a solvent-based marking pen, or scratch them into the surface with a pencil or other sharp, pointed object. Then place the Styrofoam over a block of wood for cutting with a knife or razor blade.

Styrofoam also can be cut with a coping saw, jigsaw, or scroll saw. A hot wire cutter also can be used to melt the Styrofoam and produce a smooth cut.

Styrofoam can be filed with a small surfacing tool. It also can be sanded, but not to extreme smoothness because of its cellular makeup. It is easily drilled with standard metal bits.

A number of adhesives, including epoxy, can be used for joining pieces of Styrofoam together and for joining it to other materials. However, some adhesives dissolve Styrofoam and are thus unsuitable. If in doubt, try the cement on a test strip of Styrofoam to see if it gives satisfactory results.

A variety of paints, including poster, tempera, latex, and a number of other water-based paints, can be used for painting and decorating Styrofoam. If in doubt as to whether or not a certain paint will work, try it first on a test strip.

Working with Styrofoam is generally quite easy, and this material has many possible uses for kite constructions. Styrofoam is also useful for constructing lightweight heads and other figures for use on kites.

Although Styrofoam seems to be the most readily available of the lightweight rigid-plastic foam materials, polyurethane and other types of lightweight rigid-plastic foams also can be used. The techniques for working with them are usually the same as for Styrofoam.

## Making Heads and Other Figures for Kites

Some kites, such as bird kites, use lightweight, three-dimensional shaped heads and other figures. One way to construct these figures is to carve them from Styrofoam. They then can be painted. An alternate method is to make them from lightweight papier-mâché. When this method is used, hollow out the inside of the head to keep the weight to a minimum.

## Model Airplane Techniques

Model airplane construction techniques using balsa ribs and frames and balsa sticks, can be used for constructing miniature kites, airplane kites, bird kites, and others. In general, the parts are cut from balsa wood, then glued.

The parts frequently are held in position by pins or clamps until the glue sets. Tissue or thin plastic films frequently are used as covering materials.

## Soldering

Soldering has many possibilities for advanced kite-construction work. Soldering is a method of joining metals that uses a filler metal that is called *solder*. Soldering is different from welding in that the metals being joined are not actually melted. For soldering, the melting point of the solder must be lower than that of the metal parts being joined.

To solder properly, a few basic rules should be followed:

❖ The metal surfaces to be soldered must be clean.
❖ A flux must be used that will prevent oxidation and help the flow of the solder.
❖ Enough heat must be used to melt the solder.
❖ A solder that is suitable for the particular soldering job must be used.

For metals such as tin plate, brass, and copper, a solder made from tin and lead is usually used. For general soldering of this type, a 50-50 or half tin and half lead solder that melts at about 414° Fahrenheit can be used. In most cases, a solder that has at least a 40 percent tin content should be used. Solder is sold in three basic forms: bar, solid wire, and flux-core. The *flux-core solder*, which is a hollow wire filled with flux, is generally the most convenient to use. To solder aluminum, you will need a special solder and flux.

The soldering flux is used to remove oxide films that prevent solder from adhering to the metal surfaces. The flux also lowers the surface tension of molten solder so that it can flow and penetrate properly. The two basic types of flux are rosin-base and acid or corrosive flux. For most kite construction work, the noncorrosive rosin-base flux is most suitable. In addition to flux-core solder, flux is also available in liquid and paste forms that can be brushed on before soldering.

Three types of heating devices can be used for soldering: a soldering iron, a soldering gun (both of which have copper tips), or a torch, such as a propane torch. A soldering iron is convenient for most kite construction work.

The general procedure for soldering is to clean the surfaces to be soldered with abrasive cloth or steel wool. The parts should fit closely together. If possible, clamp the parts together. The tip of the soldering iron should be clean. Heat the soldering iron and coat the copper tip with a thin layer of solder. Wipe off the excess with a damp cloth. Apply the correct flux or use a flux-core solder. Heat the metal and apply solder so that it flows into the joint.

Soldering can be used to join wire to form struts and fittings for kites, for fabricating metal fittings, and for a variety of other jobs.

# DECORATING KITES

Although some people choose to build kites purely for their flying ability, others pursue the hobby with a fascination for the beauty of kites. For some, it's the only consideration. These kite artists create kites that are works of art, not flying objects.

For our purposes, we will assume that you will be decorating kites that also can be flown. Therefore, the decoration cannot reduce the performance by adding weight or changing the balance, at least not to any great extent. The aim is to produce a kite that not only performs well, but also looks good.

## Basic Planning

Planning the decoration for a particular kite should begin early in the construction process. Some covering materials, for example, are more suitable for certain decorating techniques than others. If you want to use a painted design, you might want to cover the kite with paper. Paper is easier to paint than plastic, which is often difficult to paint.

You can decorate kites with representational designs, such as human forms, fish, trees, geometric forms, or abstract designs. Generally, if the kite itself is representational, such as a bird form, you probably also will want to decorate the kite in a representational design (that is, a bird as a bird and a dragon as a dragon, and so on). You can be realistic, with or without detail, comic, or whatever else you desire. There are really no limits.

If you choose geometric or abstract designs, you really can let your imagination go. This type of decorating is especially popular for nonfigure kites, such as the basic two-stick kite, and the hexagonal kite or other similar shapes.

Another type of decorating is to use various combinations of covering colors on the same kite. The top half of a kite, for example, could be blue and the bottom half red.

## Methods for Decorating Kites

Most kite decorating falls into one of two basic categories: using already colored materials, and adding color to materials. A combination of these methods also can be used.

**Using Colored Materials.** You can decorate a kite by selecting a covering material that is a desirable color for the particular kite. It can be a single color or a covering material that already has a design on it. For example, you can cover a kite with a silk scarf that already has a design or a representational form on it.

You can cut designs out of material of one color and paste them onto material of another color. When you do, however, you should make certain that you can join the materials securely by gluing or some other means and that the weight added to the kite will not reduce its performance to any great extent.

**Adding Color.** The most often used method for adding color is probably by painting. You can apply paint by brush, spray, or other means. Before you decorate a kite by painting, however, always try the paint you intend to use on a sample piece of the covering material to make certain that the two are compatible. Popular paints for paper-covered kites include watercolors, acrylic paints, and India ink. Special paints, marking pens, and so on are often required for plastic materials. Decorating fabrics is a skill in itself.

You can apply the paint freely, painting a design or picture on the kite-covering material. You also can use masking tape or stencils to outline the areas where you want to apply paint.

Other methods for adding color include stamping, dyeing, spatter painting, tie dyeing, batiking, and silk screening. In fact, many craft techniques for adding color to paper and other materials also can be applied to decorating kites.

Whether you add the coloring before or after you install the covering material in the kite frames depends on the technique for adding the color. In some cases, you can do the coloring or decoration either before or after you install the covering material. In other cases, as when dyeing, you usually will apply the coloring before you install the covering material on the kite frame.

## Developing Designs

Designs for decorating kites can be based on geometric figures and forms, nature, abstractions, or functional items.

**Basic Geometric Forms.** Many designs are based on geometrical figures and forms. Geometrical figures are two-dimensional; geometrical forms are three-dimensional.

The line is the simplest and most intrinsic element of geometric design. A line can be straight or curved. A straight line can be vertical, horizontal, or diagonal. As a general rule, straight lines are stronger and more direct than curved lines. The direction of the line plays an important role in strength. Vertical lines reach upward and suggest strength. Horizontal lines are more tranquil and restful. Diagonal lines suggest action.

Straight lines can be joined to form a variety of patterns. A variety of effects can be achieved. Zigzag lines, for example, give a feeling of nervous movement.

You can sketch straight lines freehand or draw them mechanically by using a straightedge or other drawing tools. Many designs start out as sketches, which are drawn without the aid of drawing tools. Naturally, sketched lines will lack precision, but with care they can be drawn adequately for the purposes of preliminary design work and even some actual kite-decorating work. Sketches are often later redrawn using drawing tools.

Lines also can be curved. A curved line is generally lighter and livelier in a design than is a straight line. You can draw curves freely by hand or make them mechanically (and sometimes mathematically) with the aid of drawing tools. You can sketch geometric figures, which are mathematical configurations, either freehand or with the aid of drawing tools. In a similar manner, you can represent three-dimensional geometric forms on paper by either sketching or mechanical drawing.

You can use a variety of geometric figures for decorating kites. A *square*, which has four equal sides meeting in right angles is a fundamental geometric figure used in decorative design. By using subdivisions, variations, and combinations of squares, you can create many designs.

A *rectangle*, which includes squares, is a four-sided figure with the sides parallel and meeting at right angles. You can form additional design patterns using other rectangular forms in addition to squares.

Triangles are important geometric figures used in design work. *Equilateral triangles* have all sides and all angles equal. A *right-angle triangle* has one right angle (an angle that has sides perpendicular to one another), two equal acute angles of 45 degrees, and two equal sides. An *isosceles triangle* has no right angle, but has two equal angles and two equal sides. A *scalene triangle* has no two sides or angles equal.

Other straight-sided figures useful in kite decorating include the rhombus, rhomboid, trapezoid, and trapezium.

You also can use curved lines to form figures that are used extensively in kite-decorating work. A *circle* is a plane figure made up of a single curved line that has every point equidistant from the point at the center.

Circles and subdivisions of circles are widely used both without and with straight lines to form design patterns. You also can form designs on kite-covering materials by making freely drawn lines.

**Designing from Natural and Man-Made Objects.** Many designs used in kite decorating are based on nature. The designs can be realistic or conventionalized (stylized). A fish form used for decorating a kite, for example, can be a representation of a particular fish, stylized to represent fish in a more general way, or even extremely stylized to be a semi-abstraction of a fish shape. In many cases, natural forms are simplified for design use.

Representations of man-made objects, such as houses, boats, automobiles, fans, and bells are other possibilities for decorating kites. Oriental and Polynesian art exhibits, books, and artifacts are all good sources of inspiration. The most important thing is to use your imagination, both to create new designs and modify traditional designs.

# FLYING KITES

Kites are flown for fun, recreation, festivals, sport, games, contests, and novelty uses. This section covers the techniques for launching, flying, landing, and using kites in a variety of ways.

## Basic Flying Techniques

Keep in mind that there is no one correct way to fly a kite. The attempt here is to present some techniques that many people have found effective.

One end of the kite string is usually attached to the bridle loop or ring on the kite, or directly to the kite, depending on the particular kite. Kite strings are usually quite long, so you will need a way to handle the string. One method is to use a cardboard tube, such as the type that string is wound on when it is sold. You also can use a wooden dowel a couple of inches in diameter or you can shape a hand reel from wood. A variety of manufactured reels that have a crank arrangement for winding the string are available.

An important consideration is a place to fly your kite. You will need a large, open space that is free of trees, electrical and telephone wires, buildings, and other obstacles. The area should be completely free of automobile traffic. The selection of the site is important for both safety and enjoyment.

To launch a kite without help, stand with your back to the wind. Hold the kite in one hand and the reel of string in the other. Let the breeze take the kite, and feed out the line. For this method to work successfully, you will need sufficient wind for the particular type of kite. Bridle angles, amount of tail, and other factors also might come into play (see Chapter 1). You also can walk toward the direction the wind is coming from as you feed out the line.

An alternate method for launching a kite is to have a partner hold the kite. This method enables you to begin with a long length of string already out.

To land a kite, you can slowly wind the string in if the wind is not too strong. You also can walk toward the kite as you reel in the line, which tends to dump the wind from the kite. In extreme conditions, you can place the reel on the ground and walk toward the kite while bringing the string in hand over hand.

You frequently will need to make adjustments to kites to get them to fly properly. The bridle angle is extremely important. If the kite won't climb, for example, you will need to reduce the bridle angle.

If the kite loops or spins uncontrollably, you can add more tail. As a general rule, you should use the minimum amount of tail that gives the kite adequate stability. Too much tail tends to make a kite heavy and sluggish.

## Ideas for Kite Flying

After you have mastered basic kite flying, you might want to go on to stunt flying and novelty kite flying. One possibility is to send *climbers* up the kite string. A piece of paper with a small hole and a slit so it can be placed over the kite string is a simple climber. The wind will carry the climber up to the kite. You also might want to design and construct other climbers in the shape of airplanes, rockets, or sailboats.

You might want to try dropping small parachutes, balloons, confetti, or messages from kites. They can be released by a string attachment or time-released, as desired.

Kites also can be used to carry up flags, banners, and other decorations. These decorations often are attached to the kite string or line some distance from the kite.

You might want to try taking photographs from kites. Attach an inexpensive camera to the kite, and use a string or time-shutter release.

You might want to try flying kites in tandem. Attach one kite to another. Usually, the smallest kite goes up first. Two or more kites can be flown in this manner.

You can use a kite for fishing. Attach a fishing line with a baited hook to the kite. Then fly the kite out over the water. It will carry the baited hook out to the desired fishing spot.

# 4
# Kite Projects

Most of the kites in this chapter are easy to construct. The more difficult kites are at the end of the chapter. If you have never built a kite, consider making the basic two-stick flat kite first. No matter what kite you would like to build, however, you must follow some general steps. These general instructions are listed first in this chapter. Following are the kite projects, with specific directions for that kite.

## GENERAL INSTRUCTIONS

❖ Dimensions given for the frame are suggested. You may vary them, as long as you keep the proportions the same. You also can use wooden dowels, sticks of fiberglass, bamboo, or aluminum tubing for the frame.

❖ Notch the ends of the sticks for the frame as shown in the illustration for that project. Then measure and mark the intersection of the frame pieces, also as illustrated.

❖ Glue and bind the frame together with string lashing, as shown in Fig. 1.

❖ Tie the ends of the string with a square knot.

❖ Apply glue to the string lashing.

❖ Install the guideline in the notches around the ends of the sticks, as shown in Fig. 1. Stretch the string tight and tie the ends together with a square knot. (If you are using fabric as a covering, do not install the guideline string until you sew the cover. Then insert the string through the sleeves in the covering.)

❖ Add lashings around the sticks on each side of the guideline strings where they pass through the notches, as shown in Fig. 1.

❖ Tie the ends of the lashings with a square knot.

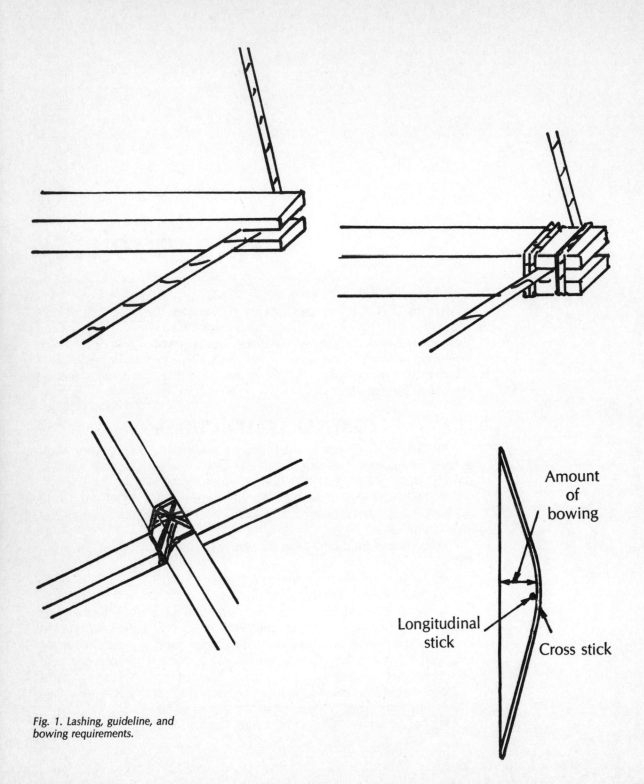

Fig. 1. Lashing, guideline, and bowing requirements.

Amount of bowing

Longitudinal stick

Cross stick

❖ Use craft-type paper or other suitable paper to cover the kite. You can use plastic film or lightweight fabric, if you choose. If you use plastic film, you can heat-seal, glue, or tape the seams. Fabric is usually sewn.

❖ Mark the pattern of the kite on the paper, using the kite frame as a pattern. Position the frame so that the side where the cross stick passes below the other sticks is against the paper.

❖ Cut the paper to the pattern (Fig. 2).

❖ Fold and glue the hems in the paper where it crosses over the ends of the sticks, as shown in Fig. 2. If you are using cloth, sew the hems and sleeves on a sewing machine or by hand. Then fold the hems and sleeves under again before sewing.

❖ Position the frame over the covering material, as shown in Fig. 3.

❖ Fold the sleeves over the guideline strings and glue the flaps to the main sections of the covering material (Fig. 3).

❖ You can paint the kite, if you desire.

❖ If you are making a bow kite, tie the bow string to one end of the cross stick, passing it through the notch in one end of the stick.

❖ Bow the stick the suggested amount (Fig. 1).

❖ Then tie the bow string to the other end of the cross stick. Notice that the longitudinal stick is inside the bow.

❖ Tie bridle strings with square knots to the ends of the sticks, passing the string through the notches.

❖ For some kites, you will need to attach the bridle strings at other places on the kite. In these instances, the strings will pass through holes in the covering material.

❖ You will need to reinforce the holes with tape or by other means.

❖ Tie the strings around the sticks at the suggested places.

❖ Use a small plastic curtain rod ring as a bridle ring and tie the bridle strings to the ring.

❖ To fly the kite, attach the kite string or line to the bridle ring. If you prefer, you can tie the strings in a loop. The ring, however, will allow you to adjust the bridle to fly the kite.

❖ You can use a variety of tails for kites. The length and weight will depend on the wind conditions when you fly the kite. You can make a basic tail from a strip of cloth approximately 6 feet long.

❖ Tie short strips of cloth to the 6-foot length at approximately 6-inch intervals.

❖ Use string to tie the tail to the kite.

❖ You also can form a tail by tying short lengths of cloth to string or by using a long strip of plastic.

❖ Generally, if a kite loops or spins, it needs more tail. Use the minimum amount required to give the kite good stability.

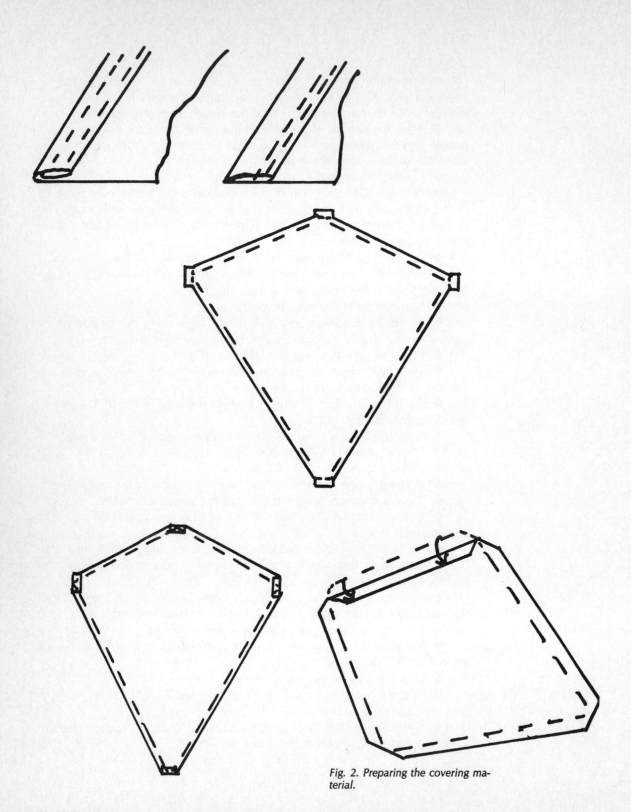

Fig. 2. Preparing the covering material.

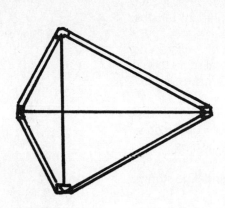

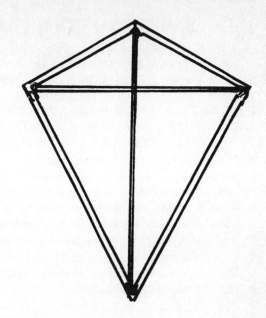

*Fig. 3. Covering the kite.*

# BASIC TWO-STICK FLAT KITE

The basic two-stick flat kite has an outline shape of four sides and two equal angles that are opposite each other. Two sides of equal length meet at each of the opposite unequal angles. Each pair of sides are of different lengths.

❖ For the frame, you will need two sticks of pine, spruce, or similar wood that are ¼ × ⅜ inch in cross section. One stick (the longitudinal stick) should be 30 inches long; the other (the cross stick) should be 36 inches long.

❖ Notch the ends of the sticks (Fig. 4).

❖ Measure and mark the intersection of the two sticks (Fig. 4). The cross stick should balance at the center point. If it does not, sand or file it until it does.

❖ Glue and bind the two sticks together with a string lashing.

❖ Install the guideline string in the notches.

❖ Add lashings around the sticks on each side of the guideline strings.

❖ Cover the frame using the material you desire.

❖ Mark the pattern for the frame on the covering material (Fig. 4).

❖ Cut the paper to the pattern.

❖ Fold and glue or sew the hems in the paper.

❖ Position the frame over the covering material.

❖ Fold the sleeves over the guideline strings.

❖ Glue the flaps to the main sections of the covering material.

❖ Tie the bridle strings to the ends of the sticks.

❖ Tie the other end of the string to a bridle ring.

❖ To make the tail, use a 6-foot-long piece of cloth. Tie short lengths of cloth at 6-inch intervals.

**Variations**. A number of interesting variations of the basic two-stick flat kite are possible. By keeping the proportions approximately the same, you can make the kite very large. Use a 5-foot-long cross stick and a 6-foot-long longitudinal stick.

If you use balsa for the sticks, you can construct the kite in miniature using a longitudinal stick of 1 foot or less in length.

You probably would want to cover large kites with fabric or plastic material. You can use a very thin tissue paper or plastic film to cover small kites.

One problem with an extremely large two-stick flat kite is that a large tail is usually required to give it adequate stability. For this reason, if you want to make a large two-stick flat kite, the bowed model, detailed next, is recommended.

You also might want to experiment with length-to-breadth proportions or placement of the cross stick on the longitudinal stick.

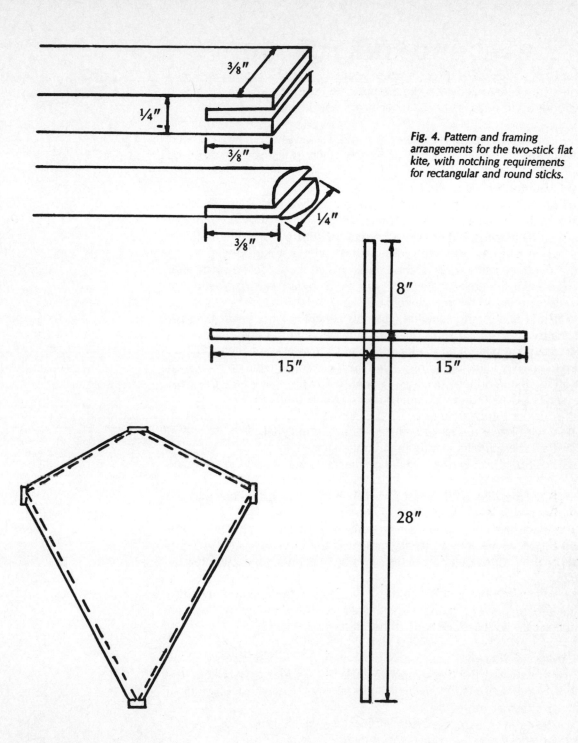

*Fig. 4.* Pattern and framing arrangements for the two-stick flat kite, with notching requirements for rectangular and round sticks.

3/8″

1/4″

3/8″

3/8″

1/4″

8″

15″    15″

28″

# BASIC TWO-STICK BOW KITE

The basic two-stick bow kite is sometimes called an *Eddy kite* because it was invented by William Eddy. Unlike the basic two-stick flat kite, this kite will fly without a tail because of its wider beam and its bow.

❖ You will need two sticks for the frame, ¼ × ⅜ inch in cross section and 36 inches in length. Wooden dowels ⁵⁄₁₆ inch in diameter also can be used.

❖ Notch the ends of the sticks.

❖ Measure and mark the intersection on the two sticks (Fig. 5). Make sure the cross stick balances at the center point and that it forms an even bow when bent by its ends. If it does not, correct the stick by sanding and filing.

❖ Glue and bind the two sticks together with a string lashing.

❖ If you are using a sewn fabric cover, install the guideline string after you have sewn the cover material. If you are using a paper or plastic film covering material, install the guideline now.

❖ Cloth and plastic covering materials generally work better than paper because they stretch sufficiently to allow the kite to bow.

❖ Mark the pattern on the fabric, using the frame as a pattern (Fig. 5). Place a temporary guideline string around the frame through the notches, then position the frame on the covering material so that the side where the cross stick passes below the longitudinal stick is against the fabric.

❖ Cut out the pattern.

❖ Glue or sew the hems and sleeves in the material.

❖ Pass the guideline string through the sleeves.

❖ Position the covering material on the frame and install the guideline string.

❖ Bow the kite until it has a 4-inch bow (Fig. 5). Notice that the longitudinal stick is inside the bow.

❖ Attach the upper bridle string to the two sticks where they join. It should be 24 inches long to its attachment at the bridle ring.

❖ Make a reinforced hole in the covering material for the string to pass through.

❖ Attach the lower string to the lower end of the longitudinal stick, passing it through the notch in the end of the stick. This string should be about 36 inches long to its attachment at the bridle ring.

**Variations.** There are many possible variations to the basic two-stick bow kite. You can make the design smaller or larger, as long as you keep the proportions the same. This design is suitable for large sizes with a longitudinal length of 6 feet or more.

You also might want to experiment by changing the proportional length of the two sticks and the placement of the cross joint.

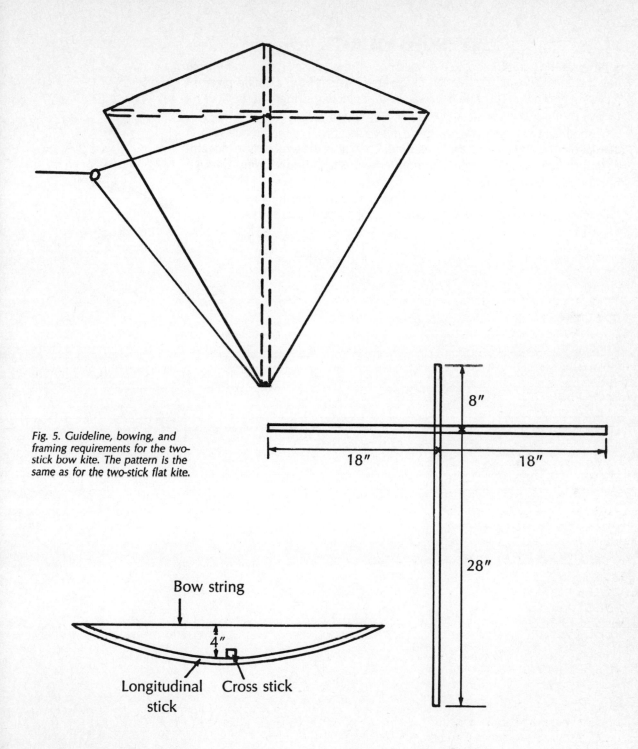

Fig. 5. Guideline, bowing, and framing requirements for the two-stick bow kite. The pattern is the same as for the two-stick flat kite.

8"

18"     18"

28"

Bow string

4"

Longitudinal stick     Cross stick

# STYROFOAM KITE

An interesting variation of the two-stick bow kite is to use Styrofoam for both the frame and covering material. One version is cut from a single piece of ½-inch Styrofoam. This kite is bowed with a piece of string. The bow string passes through reinforced holes in the Styrofoam.

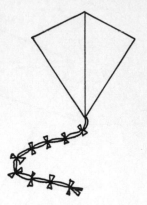

Another Styrofoam version is made in two sections (Fig. 6). Cut one section at a 12-degree angle along the centerline. Then glue the two sections together to form a 12-degree angle at the centerline. Attach bridle strings through holes in the Styrofoam.

For stability, Styrofoam kites usually need a tail. You might want to try other sizes and shapes, such as round, square, and figure forms.

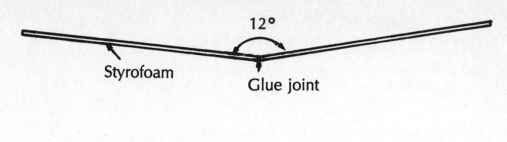

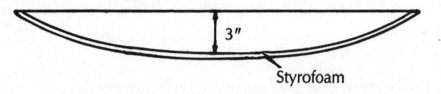

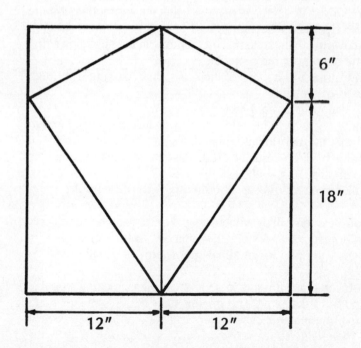

Fig. 6. Joining, bowing, and framing arrangements for the Styrofoam kite.

# THREE-STICK KITE
# WITH CONVERGING LONGITUDINALS

The three-stick kite with converging longitudinals can be made with or without a bow. Its performance is generally improved by the addition of a bow string.

❖ You will need three 36-inch-long sticks for the frame. You can use wooden dowels with a diameter of ¼ inch, or sticks with a cross section of ¼ × ⅜ inch.

❖ At the ends of the sticks, make saw cuts to a depth of ⅜ inch. Make certain that the notches line up at the ends of each stick.

❖ Measure and mark the intersections as shown in Fig. 7.

❖ Use string to glue and lash the two longitudinal sticks to the cross stick.

❖ Glue and tie the two longitudinals together.

❖ Insert a piece of metal or plastic that will just fit in the notches to keep the notches lined up until the glue sets.

❖ Install the guideline string and add lashings.

❖ Mark the pattern for the covering as shown in Fig. 7, using the kite frame, with either the permanent or a temporary guideline string, as a pattern.

❖ Cut the covering material to the pattern, using the appropriate joining method to form the sleeves and hem.

❖ Install the covering material to the kite frame with the guideline string passing through the sleeves in the material.

❖ Tie the bow string to one end of the cross stick, passing it through the notch in the end of the stick.

❖ Bow the kite until it has a 4-inch bow.

❖ Tie the bow string to the other end of the cross stick, passing it through the notch. Notice that the two longitudinal sticks are inside the bow.

❖ A three-string bridle is usually used. Pass the strings through the notches and tie them around the ends of the sticks.

❖ Use a small curtain rod ring as a bridle ring and tie the bridle strings to the ring.

❖ This type of kite often will fly without a tail. For some flying conditions, however, you might need a tail. A single tail attached to the bottom end of the kite frame—where the two longitudinal sticks join—is usually used.

**Variations**. You can make this kite in a variety of sizes, making sure that you keep the proportions the same. The smaller sizes require smaller sticks and lightweight covering materials; the larger sizes require larger sticks and heavier covering materials. You also might want to experiment with the proportions.

You can fly the kite without a bow if you use a tail, but the performance is considerably improved by the addition of a bow string.

Fig. 7. Pattern and framing requirements for the three-stick kite with converging longitudinals.

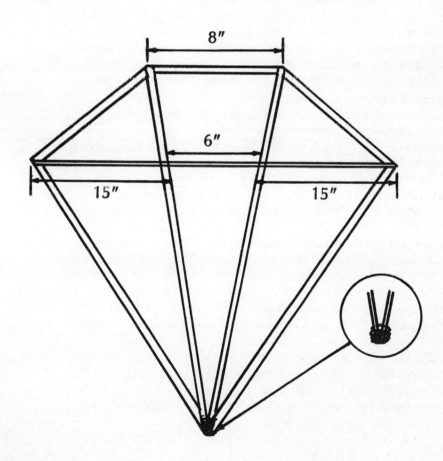

# THREE-STICK KITE
# WITH PARALLEL LONGITUDINALS

This kite can be used with or without a bow, as desired. A bow, however, will improve the kite's performance and often will eliminate the need for a tail.

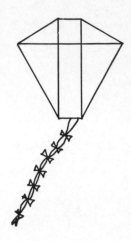

❖ You will need three sticks for the frame, each 36 inches long and with a cross section of ¼ × ⅜ inch (Fig. 8). Wooden dowels having a diameter of ¼ inch are another possibility.

❖ Notch both ends of all three sticks to a depth of ⅜ inch. Make sure the notches are in the same plane.

❖ Measure and mark the intersections on each stick (Fig. 8).

❖ Glue and lash the two longitudinal sticks to the cross stick.

❖ Tie the ends of the strings together with square knots. Again, make sure all the notches are parallel to the plane surface of the kite.

❖ Install the guideline string in the notches (Fig. 8).

❖ Add lashings around the sticks on each side of the guideline string, where it passes through the notches in the sticks.

❖ You can use paper, plastic, or cloth to cover the kite. Mark the pattern shown in Fig. 8 on the material.

❖ Cut the covering material to the pattern, using the appropriate joining method to form the sleeves and hem.

❖ Install the covering material on the kite frame with the guideline string passing through sleeves in the material.

❖ Bow the kite until it has a 4-inch bow. The two longitudinal sticks should be inside the bow.

❖ A four-string bridle is usually used with this type of kite. Pass the strings through the notches and tie them around the ends of the sticks.

❖ Tie the bridle strings to the bridle ring, adjusting for particular flying conditions.

❖ Two tails are usually used with this kite. Attach them to the aft ends of the longitudinal sticks. The length and weight of the tails will depend on the wind conditions and other factors.

**Variations.** The three-stick kite with parallel longitudinals can be made in a variety of sizes from 1 foot or less in length and breadth to 6 feet or more, keeping the proportions the same. For use in light air, sticks with smaller cross section than that given can be used. For use in very strong winds, you might need larger cross sections to give the kite frame adequate strength.

You also might want to experiment by changing the proportions of the kite, such as the width between the two longitudinal sticks, or the distance from the top of the kite to the cross stick.

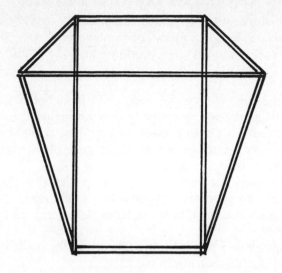

Fig. 8. Pattern, framing, and guideline requirements for the three-stick kite with parallel longitudinals.

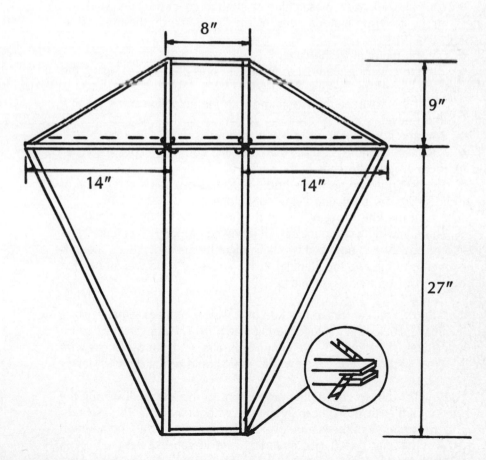

8"

9"

14"

14"

27"

# THREE-STICK KITE
# WITH CROSSING LONGITUDINALS

The three-stick kite with crossing longitudinals can be flown without a bow string if tails are used. The use of a bow string, however, usually improves the kite's performance, and often gives good performance even if tails are not used.

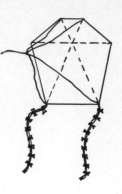

❖ You will need three sticks for the frame: two 36 inches long and one 30 inches long. You can use wooden sticks with a rectangular cross section of ¼ × ⅜ inch or round wooden dowels with a diameter of ¼ inch.

❖ Cut a ⅜-inch-deep notch in each end of all three sticks, making sure the notches on both ends of a stick are in the same plane.

❖ Measure and mark the intersections on each stick (Fig. 9).

❖ Glue and lash all three sticks together in a single joint.

❖ Install the guideline string in the notches at the ends of the sticks around the kite frame (Fig. 9).

❖ Add lashings around the sticks on each side of the guideline string where it passes through the notches in the sticks.

❖ You can use paper, plastic film, or cloth to cover the kite. Mark the pattern on the covering material, placing the kite frame on the material as a pattern (Fig. 9).

❖ Cut the material to the pattern.

❖ Join the covering material to form the hems and sleeves, using the appropriate method for the material used.

❖ Install the cover to the kite frame with the guideline string passing through the sleeves.

❖ Bow the kite until it has a 3½-inch bow.

❖ A four-string bridle is usually used. Pass the strings through the notches and tie them around the ends of the sticks.

❖ Tie the bridle strings to the bridle ring. You can adjust the length of the bridle strings for particular flying conditions.

❖ Attach the kite string or line to the bridle ring for flying the kite.

❖ This kite will fly without a tail if it is bowed properly. In certain flying conditions, however, a bow and two tails might be needed. Attach the tails to the aft ends of the two longitudinal sticks. The length and weight needed will depend on the flying conditions.

**Variations.** You can make this kite in a variety of sizes. Smaller sizes require smaller sticks and lighter covering materials. The converse is true for the larger sizes. If you will fly the kite in light airs, you can use sticks with smaller cross sections. For strong winds, you should use sticks with larger cross sections.

You might want to change the proportions of the kite by lowering the intersection of the sticks. You can fly the kite without a bow if you use tails.

The performance of the kite is considerably improved with the addition of a bow string, and one is recommended even if you use tails.

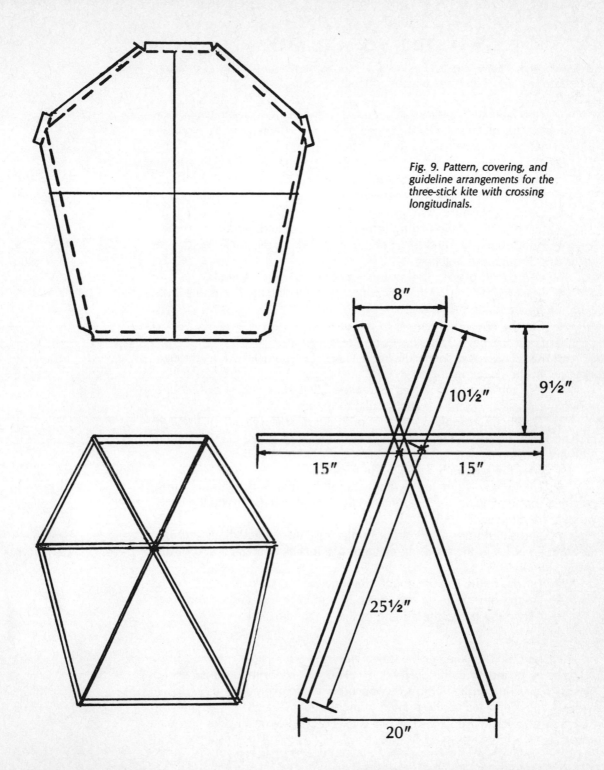

*Fig. 9. Pattern, covering, and guideline arrangements for the three-stick kite with crossing longitudinals.*

8"

10½"

9½"

15"

15"

25½"

20"

# TWO-STICK SQUARE KITE

The two-stick square kite can be flown with or without a bow string, as desired. The kite usually requires a tail for adequate stability.

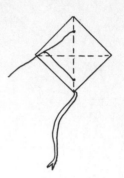

❖ Two 24-inch-long sticks are required for the frame. You can use wooden sticks with a rectangular cross section of ³⁄₁₆ × ⁵⁄₁₆ inch or round wooden dowels with a diameter of ³⁄₁₆ inch.

❖ Cut notches in both ends of the sticks to a depth of ³⁄₈ inch. Make sure the notches on both ends are in the same plane.

❖ Measure and mark the center point on each stick (Fig. 10).

❖ Glue and lash the two sticks together.

❖ Install the guideline string in the notches around the kite frame.

❖ Add lashings around the sticks on each side of the guideline where it passes through the notches.

❖ Use paper, plastic film, or cloth as the covering material.

❖ Mark the pattern on the covering material, using the kite frame with guideline as a pattern (Fig. 10).

❖ Cut the covering material to the pattern.

❖ Form the hems and sleeves on the covering.

❖ Install the cover on the kite frame, passing the guideline string through sleeves in the covering.

❖ Use the stick that passes under the other stick and is against the covering material where the sticks cross as the cross stick.

❖ Tie the bow string to one end of the cross stick, passing it through the notch in the end of the stick so that it cannot slide down the stick when the kite is bowed.

❖ Bow the kite until it has a 3-inch bow.

❖ Tie the bow string to the other end of the cross stick with the string passing through the notch. The longitudinal stick should be inside the bow, above the cross stick.

❖ You should use a two-string bridle. Pass the bridle strings through reinforced holes in the covering material 4½ inches from each end of the longitudinal stick.

❖ Tie the bridle strings around the longitudinal stick.

❖ Tie the other ends of the strings in a loop or to a curtain rod ring.

❖ Attach the tail to the aft end of the longitudinal stick.

**Variations.** This kite can be flown with one of the sides instead of the corners as the top. With this position, it will be a flat kite without a bow string. Use a four-string bridle with the connections at each corner, and two tails, which are connected to the bottom corners.

You also can construct the kite in a variety of sizes, as detailed for previous projects.

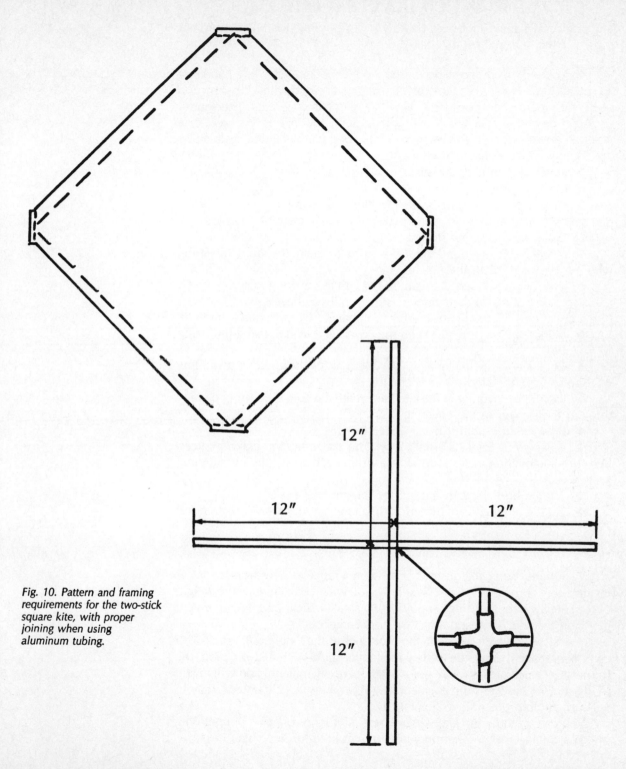

Fig. 10. Pattern and framing
requirements for the two-stick
square kite, with proper
joining when using
aluminum tubing.

12"

12"

12"

12"

# TWO-STICK DIAMOND KITE

The two-stick diamond kite can be flown with or without a bow string, but a tail is usually needed for stability.

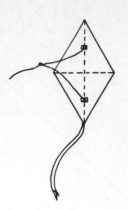

❖ You will need two sticks for the frame: one 36 inches long, and one 24 inches long. The longer stick can be rectangular wood with a cross section of ¼ × ⅜ inch, or a wooden dowel with a diameter of ¼ inch. The shorter stick can be rectangular wood with a cross section of ³⁄₁₆ × ⁵⁄₁₆ inch, or a wooden dowel with a diameter of ³⁄₁₆ inch. For a particular kite, both sticks are usually either rectangular or round.

❖ Notch the ends of the sticks to a depth of ⅜ inch.

❖ Measure and mark the center point on each stick (Fig. 11).

❖ Glue and lash the two sticks together with string. Position all of the end notches so that they are parallel to the plane surface of the kite.

❖ Install the guideline string in the notches around the kite frame.

❖ Install lashings around the sticks on each side of the guideline string where it passes through the notches.

❖ You can use paper, plastic film, or cloth as covering material. If you use cloth, do not install the guideline string until you have sewn the cover. Use a covering with the lightest weight compatible with adequate strength.

❖ Mark the pattern (Fig. 11) on the covering material, using the frame as a guide.

❖ Cut the covering material to the pattern, using the appropriate joining method to form the sleeves and hem.

❖ Install the covering to the kite frame with the guideline string passing through the sleeves in the covering.

❖ Bow the kite until it has a 3-inch bow.

❖ A two-string bridle is usually used. Pass the strings through reinforced holes in the covering material 8½ inches from each end of the longitudinal stick.

❖ Tie the bridle strings around the longitudinal stick.

❖ Tie the other ends of the strings in a loop or onto a small curtain-rod ring.

❖ Attach the tail to the aft end of the longitudinal stick.

**Variations.** You can construct this kite in a range of sizes from 1 foot or less to 6 feet or more in length. Generally, you will need to reduce the weight of the smaller sizes by using proportionally smaller sticks and lighter weight covering material. The opposite is true for larger sticks.

You also can fly the kite with the short stick as the longitudinal stick. You can either make it a flat kite or bow the longer stick. With this variation, the bridle strings will pass through holes in the covering material and will attach to the stick 4½ inches from each end. A single tail is usually used, but three tails are another possibility. (See Fig. 12.)

You can try to fly the kite without a tail. If it loops or spins uncontrollably, use a tail. Use the minimum amount required for good stability.

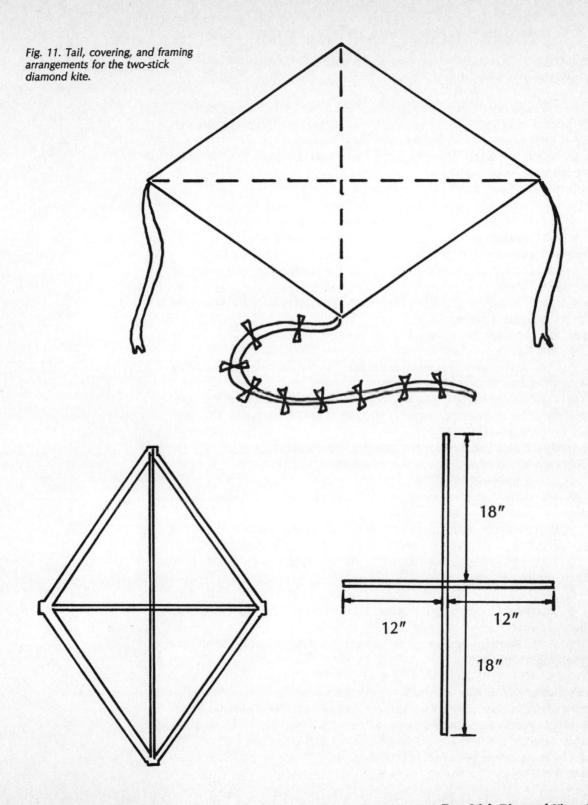

Fig. 11. Tail, covering, and framing arrangements for the two-stick diamond kite.

18″

12″    12″

18″

# THREE-STICK HEXAGONAL KITE

The three-stick hexagonal kite can be used as a flat or bowed kite. A tail is usually needed for stability.

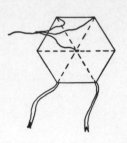

❖ You will need three 36-inch-long sticks to make the frame. Wooden sticks with a rectangular cross section of ³⁄₁₆ × ⁵⁄₁₆ inch or round wooden dowels with a diameter of ³⁄₁₆ inch are good choices.

❖ Notch the ends of the sticks ³⁄₈ inch deep; be careful to keep the notches in the same plane.

❖ Measure and mark the center point on each stick (Fig. 12).

❖ Glue and lash the three sticks together with string.

❖ Install the guideline string in the end notches of the sticks.

❖ Add lashings around the sticks on each side of the guideline, where it passes through the notches.

❖ Use the lightest-weight covering material compatible with adequate strength.

❖ Mark the pattern (Fig. 12) on the covering material, using the kite frame with guideline as a pattern.

❖ Cut the covering material to the pattern.

❖ Join the sleeves and hems.

❖ Install the covering material to the kite frame with the guideline string passing through the sleeves in the covering.

❖ Tie the bow string to one end of the stick that passes under the other two sticks and is against the covering material at the center point. This stick will be the cross stick.

❖ Pass the string through the notch and on around the stick.

❖ Bow the kite until it has a 4½-inch bow (Fig. 12).

❖ Use a three-string bridle.

❖ The upper two attachments are to the upper ends of the longitudinal sticks.

❖ Pass the center attachment through a hole in the center of the covering material and tie it around the center points of the longitudinal sticks.

❖ Each string should be about 20 inches long from the points of attachment on the kite.

❖ Tie the loose ends of the strings in a loop or to a small plastic ring.

❖ Two tails are often used, attached to the aft ends of the two longitudinal sticks.

❖ If you want to use a single tail, attach it to a string tied to the aft ends of the longitudinal sticks.

**Variations.** You can construct this kite in a range of sizes. Reduce the weight of the smaller sizes by using proportionally smaller sticks and lighter covering material. Use larger sticks and heavier material for the larger sizes.

You can fly the hexagonal kite with points at the top and bottom. You also can use a bridle with two points of attachment. If you prefer, you can attach three tails.

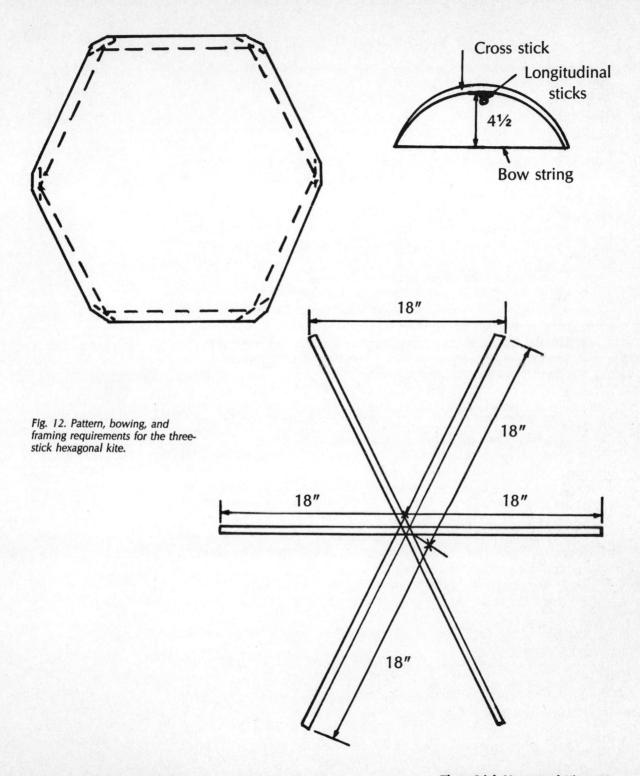

Cross stick

Longitudinal sticks

4½

Bow string

18″

18″

18″

18″

18″

Fig. 12. Pattern, bowing, and framing requirements for the three-stick hexagonal kite.

# BASIC THREE-STICK KITE

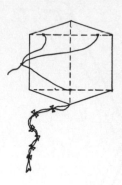

The three-stick kite is similar to the basic two-stick kite. An exception is that a second cross stick, equal in length to the first one, is added. You can use the kite flat or bowed. A tail is usually required.

❖ Use three 36-inch-long sticks for the frame. You can use a wooden stick with a rectangular cross section of ¼ × ⅜ inch, or a round wooden dowel with a diameter of ¼ inch. For the cross sticks, use two wooden sticks with a rectangular cross section of ³⁄₁₆ × ⁵⁄₁₆ inch or round wood dowels with diameters of ³⁄₁₆ inch.

❖ Notch the ends of each stick by making a saw cut to a depth of ⅜ inch.

❖ Measure and mark the center point on each cross stick (Fig. 13).

❖ Measure and mark points 6 inches from each end of the longitudinal stick (Fig. 13).

❖ Glue and lash the sticks together with string.

❖ Install the guideline string around the kite frame.

❖ Add lashings around the sticks on each side of the guideline string where it passes through the notches.

❖ Use the lightest weight of covering material to give adequate strength.

❖ Mark the pattern shown in Fig. 13 on the covering material.

❖ Cut the covering material to the pattern.

❖ Join the covering material to form the hems and sleeves.

❖ Install the cover with the guideline string passing through sleeves in the material.

❖ Use two bow strings, one on each cross stick.

❖ Bow the cross sticks 4½ inches. The longitudinal stick should be inside the bow, above the cross sticks.

❖ A three-string bridle is usually used. The upper two attachments are to the upper cross stick, 6 inches from each end, with the strings passed through reinforced holes in the covering material and tied around the stick.

❖ The other attachment is to the cross point of the lower cross stick and the longitudinal stick. Pass the string through a reinforced hole in the covering material and tie it around the sticks.

❖ Tie the other ends of the strings in a loop or to a small curtain rod ring.

❖ Use a single tail. Attach it to the aft end of the longitudinal stick.

**Variations.** You can use three tails. You also can attach two tails to the aft end of the sticks.

You can construct the kite in a range of sizes, always keeping the proportions the same, and using the appropriate weight of covering material.

You can fly the kite with one of the flat sides downward. You also can use a bridle with four points of attachment.

You can place the cross sticks at different points on the longitudinal stick, also. You can make the lower cross stick shorter than the upper one (Fig. 14).

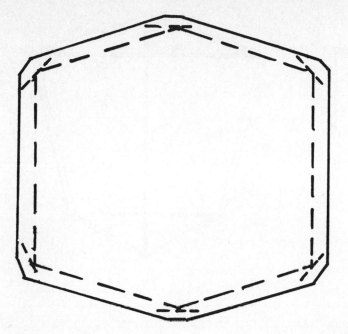

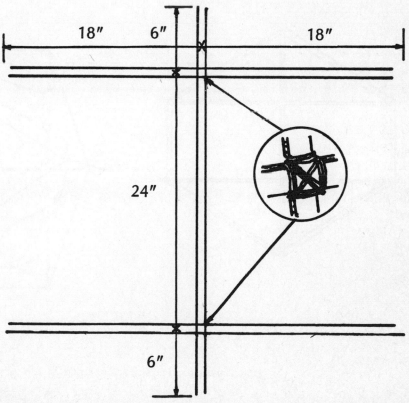

Fig. 13. Pattern and framing requirements, with lashings, for the basic three-stick kite.

18"    6"    18"

24"

6"

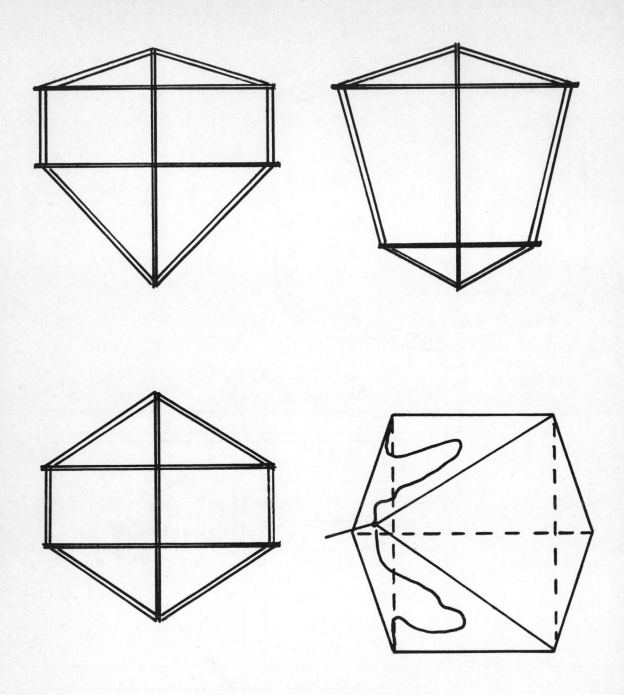

Fig. 14. Framing and bridle variations for the basic three-stick kite.

# RECTANGULAR KITE

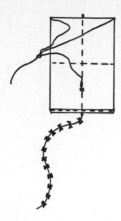

The rectangular kite can be used with or without a bow. It does need a tail to give it adequate stability.

❖ You will need one stick 36 inches long and three sticks 24 inches long for the frame (Fig. 15). For the longitudinal stick, you can use a wooden stick with a cross section of ¼ × ⅜ inch, or a round wooden dowel with a diameter of ¼ inch. For the cross sticks, use sticks with a cross section of ³⁄₁₆ × ⁵⁄₁₆ inch or round wooden dowels with a diameter of ³⁄₁₆ inch.

❖ Carve grooves in the ends of the cross sticks for the guideline strings.

❖ Measure and mark the center point on each cross stick (Fig. 15).

❖ Measure and mark points 1½ inches from each end of the longitudinal stick.

❖ Glue and lash the sticks together with string.

❖ Attach the guideline strings to the ends of the cross sticks in the grooves. Stretch the two strings tight so they hold the cross sticks in the proper positions.

❖ Tie each guideline string to the upper and lower cross sticks with square knots. You will need to install the upper cross stick in the upper sleeve before gluing and binding the stick to the longitudinal stick.

❖ Mark the pattern in Fig. 15 on the covering material. The bottom of the covering material has a hem only and does not form a sleeve.

❖ Cut the covering material to the pattern, using the appropriate joining method to form the sleeves and hem.

❖ Install the covering material to the kite frame with the guideline strings and upper cross stick passing through sleeves.

❖ You can add a bow string to the upper cross stick, and to the center cross stick if desired.

❖ Bow the cross stick until it has a 3-inch bow.

❖ If you want to use a bow string on the center cross stick, attach it in the same way you did for the upper cross stick.

❖ The longitudinal stick should be inside the bow.

❖ You can use a three-string bridle. The upper two attachments are to the grooves at the ends of the upper cross stick. The other attachment is to the longitudinal stick 9 inches from the lower end.

❖ Pass the string through a reinforced hole in the covering material and tie it around the stick.

❖ Tie the remaining ends in a loop or to a curtain rod ring.

❖ You can use a single tail. Attach it to the aft end of the longitudinal stick at the intersection of the lower cross stick.

**Variations.** You can add three tails.

You can construct the kite in a range of sizes from 1 foot or less to over 6 feet, keeping the proportions the same. Reduce the weight of the smaller sizes by using lighter weight covering materials. Use heavier covering material for the larger sizes.

You can use a variety of other framing arrangements, also (Fig. 16).

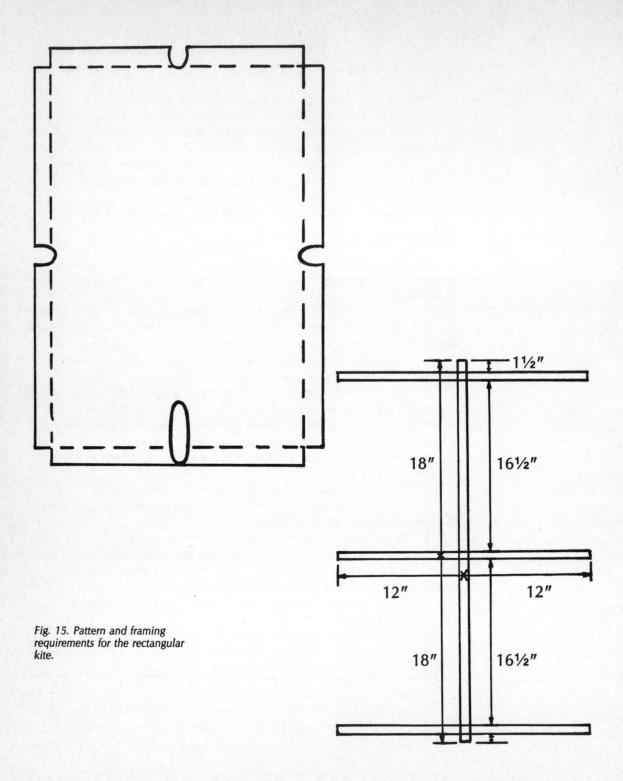

Fig. 15. Pattern and framing requirements for the rectangular kite.

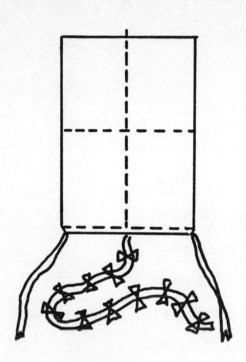

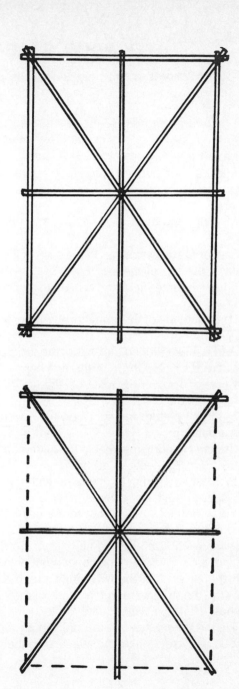

Fig. 16. Tail and framing variations for the rectangular kite.

# FIVE-POINT STAR KITE

The five-point star kite is usually used as a flat kite. A tail is needed for adequate stability.

❖ You will need three 36-inch-long sticks to make the frame. You can use wooden sticks with a rectangular cross section of ¼ × ⅜ inch or round wooden dowels with a diameter of ¼ inch.

❖ Make a ⅜-inch-deep notch in the ends of the sticks, except the two ends that meet at the point at the top of the star. Make the notches on both ends of each stick in the same plane.

❖ Measure and mark the points of attachment for the sticks, as shown in Fig. 17.

❖ Saw or file cross notches in the ends of the two sticks where they meet in a point at the top of the star (Fig. 17).

❖ Glue the three sticks and lash them together with string to the pattern in Fig. 17.

❖ Pass the ends of the string through the notches and tie them around the sticks.

❖ Add lashings around the ends of the sticks on each side of the guideline strings where they pass through the notches.

❖ Choose a covering material that is as light as possible without sacrificing strength.

❖ Mark the pattern in Fig. 17 on the covering material, using the kite frame as a pattern.

❖ Cut the covering material to the pattern, using the appropriate joining method to form the sleeves and hem.

❖ Install the covering to the frame with the guideline strings and frame sticks passing through the sleeves.

❖ You can add a bow string to the cross stick if you desire. The kite will need a 4-inch bow.

❖ A three-string bridle is usually used. The upper attachment is to the cross joint of the two sticks at the upper point of the star. The two lower strings attach to the aft ends of the two longitudinal sticks.

❖ Wrap the strings around the ends of the sticks, passing them through the notches. Tie them with square knots.

❖ Tie the other ends of the strings in a loop or to a small plastic ring.

❖ You can use a single tail attached to the aft ends of the longitudinal sticks.

**Variations.** You can use two tails. Attach them to the aft ends of the longitudinal sticks.

You can construct the kite in a range of sizes. Keep the proportions the same.

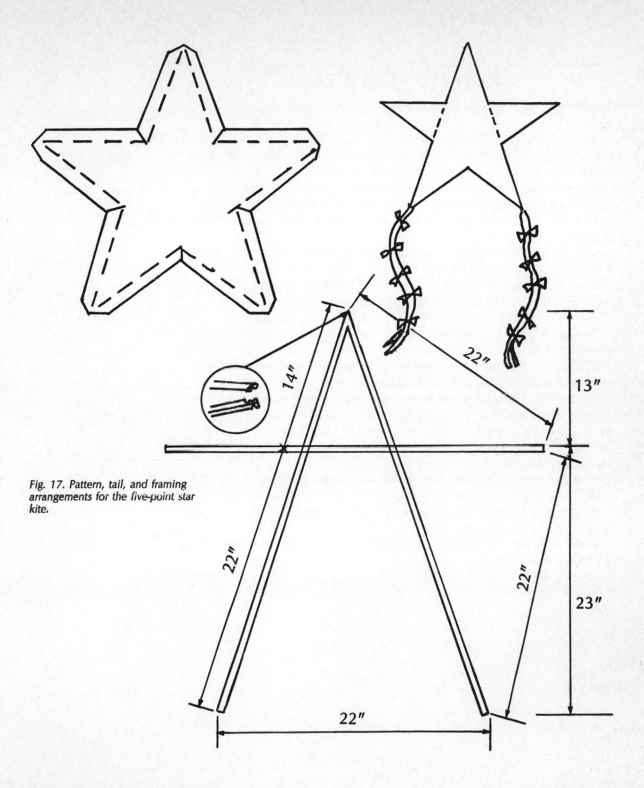

Fig. 17. Pattern, tail, and framing arrangements for the five-point star kite.

14"

22"

22"

22"

22"

22"

13"

23"

# SIX-POINT STAR KITE

This kite is usually used as a flat kite. It needs a tail for stability.

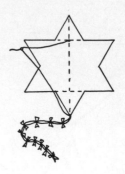

❖ You need one 36-inch-long stick and two 32-inch-long sticks for the frame. Wooden sticks with a rectangular cross section of ¼ × ⅜ inch or round wooden dowels with a diameter of ¼ inch are your choices.

❖ Make ⅜-inch-deep notches in the ends of the sticks. Make sure the notches on both sides of each stick are in the same plane.

❖ Measure and mark the points of attachment for the sticks as shown in Fig. 18.

❖ Glue the sticks and lash them together with string to the pattern shown.

❖ Use two guideline strings.

❖ Add lashing strings around the ends of the sticks on each side of the guideline strings where they pass through the notches.

❖ Mark the pattern in Fig. 18 on the covering.

❖ Cut the covering material to the pattern, using the appropriate joining method to form the sleeves and hem.

❖ Install the covering to the frame, with the guideline strings and frame sticks passing through sleeves in the material.

❖ You can add bow strings to the cross sticks. Bow the sticks until they have a 3½-inch bow.

❖ A two-string bridle can be used. The upper attachment is to the cross joint of the upper cross stick and longitudinal stick. Pass the string through a small reinforced hole in the covering material.

❖ The lower attachment is to the aft end of the longitudinal stick.

❖ Tie the other ends of the strings in a loop or to a plastic ring.

❖ Attach a single tail to the aft end of the longitudinal stick.

**Variations.** You can construct the kite in a range of sizes. Be sure to keep the proportions the same.

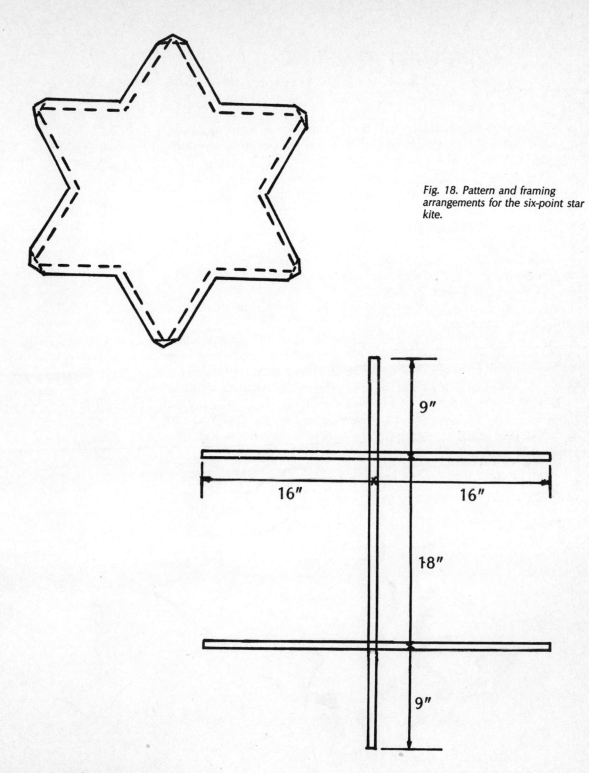

Fig. 18. Pattern and framing arrangements for the six-point star kite.

9"

16"

16"

18"

9"

# EIGHT-POINT STAR KITE

The eight-point star kite is usually used as a flat kite. It needs a tail for adequate stability.

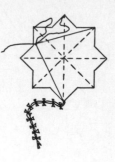

❖ You will need four 36-inch-long sticks for the frame. You can use either wooden sticks with a cross section of ³⁄₁₆ × ⁵⁄₁₆ inch, or round wooden dowels with a diameter of ³⁄₁₆ inch.

❖ Cut a ³⁄₈-inch notch in the ends of the sticks.

❖ Measure and mark the center points of each stick (Fig. 19).

❖ Glue the sticks and lash them together with string.

❖ Use two guideline strings (Fig. 20).

❖ Add lashings.

❖ Mark the pattern in Fig. 19 on the covering material.

❖ Cut the material to the pattern, using the appropriate joining method to form the sleeves and hem.

❖ Attach the covering to the frame with the guideline strings passing through sleeves in the material.

❖ A four-string bridle can be used. The upper three attachments are to the upper ends of the sticks that form the upper star points. The lower attachment is to the aft end of the longitudinal center stick.

❖ You can attach a single tail to the aft end of the longitudinal stick.

**Variations.** You can use three tails, if you desire. (See Fig. 20.) You also can vary the size of the kite from 1 foot to 6 feet. Be sure to keep the proportions the same.

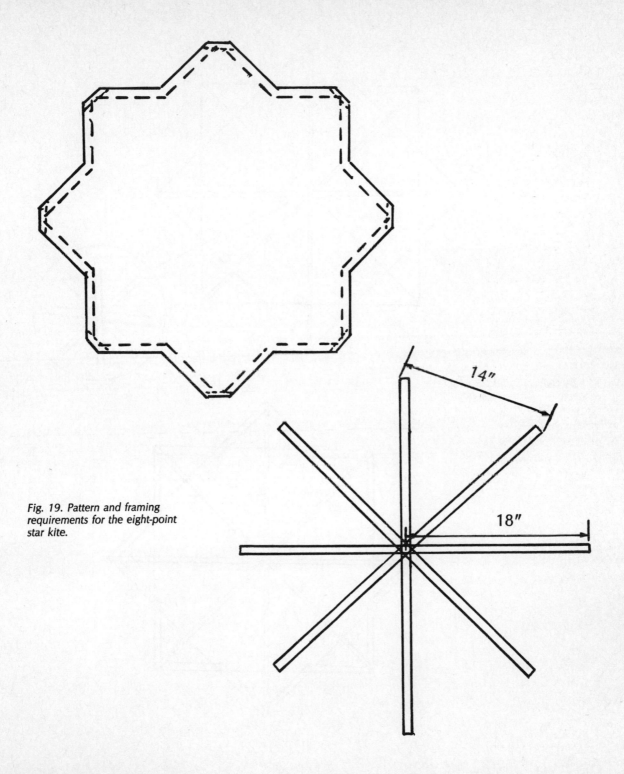

Fig. 19. Pattern and framing requirements for the eight-point star kite.

14"

18"

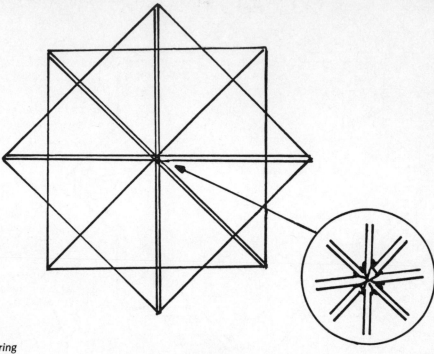

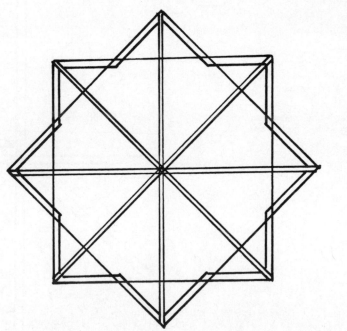

*Fig. 20. Guideline and covering requirements for the eight-point star kite.*

# ARCH-TOP KITE

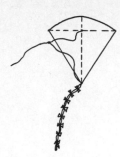

The arch-top kite can be used with or without a bow. It does, however, require a tail for stability.

❖ You need three sticks for the frame. Use wooden sticks with cross sections of ¼ × ⅜ inch or wooden dowels with diameters of ¼ inch for the longitudinal and cross stick. The longitudinal stick is 36 inches long and the cross stick is 32 inches long.

❖ A wooden dowel ⅛ inch round and 36 inches long is needed for the arch stick. You also can use a bamboo strip 36 inches long.

❖ Notch the aft end of the longitudinal stick, cutting to a depth of ⅜ inch.

❖ Measure and mark the center point of the cross and arch sticks (Fig. 21).

❖ Measure and mark points 1 inch and 9 inches from the top end of the longitudinal stick (Fig. 21).

❖ Glue and lash the center of the arch stick to the longitudinal stick 1 inch from the top, tying with a square knot.

❖ Bend the arch stick and glue and bind it to the ends of the cross stick, with 1-inch extensions of each stick (Fig. 21), again using square knots.

❖ Add a guideline string. Tie one end of the string to the cross joint of the cross stick and arch stick at one end of the cross stick. Pass the string downward and through the notch in the aft end of the longitudinal stick. Extend it upward and tie it to the cross joint of the cross stick and arch stick at the other end of the cross stick.

❖ Stretch the string tight and adjust the tension until it pulls the cross stick straight and balances the tension between the arch stick and the guideline string.

❖ Tie the guideline string with a square knot.

❖ Add a lashing string around the aft end of the longitudinal stick on both sides of the guideline string where it passes through the notch.

❖ Tie the ends together with a square knot. You might want to wait to install the arch stick through the sleeve in the covering material before you attach the stick to the kite frame.

❖ Mark the pattern in Fig. 21 on the covering material. Notice that the covering material has sleeves for both the arch stick and the guideline string.

❖ Cut the covering material to the pattern, using the appropriate joining method to form the sleeves and hem.

❖ Attach the cover to the frame with the guideline string and arch stick passing through sleeves in the cover.

❖ Tie a bow string to the cross joint of the cross stick and arch stick at one end of the cross stick.

❖ Wrap the string through the V formed by the sticks.

❖ Bow the stick until it has a 4-inch bow.

❖ Use a two-string bridle. The upper attachment is through a hole in the covering material (which should be reinforced) at the point where the longitudinal and cross sticks join.

❖ Tie the string around the joint of the two sticks.

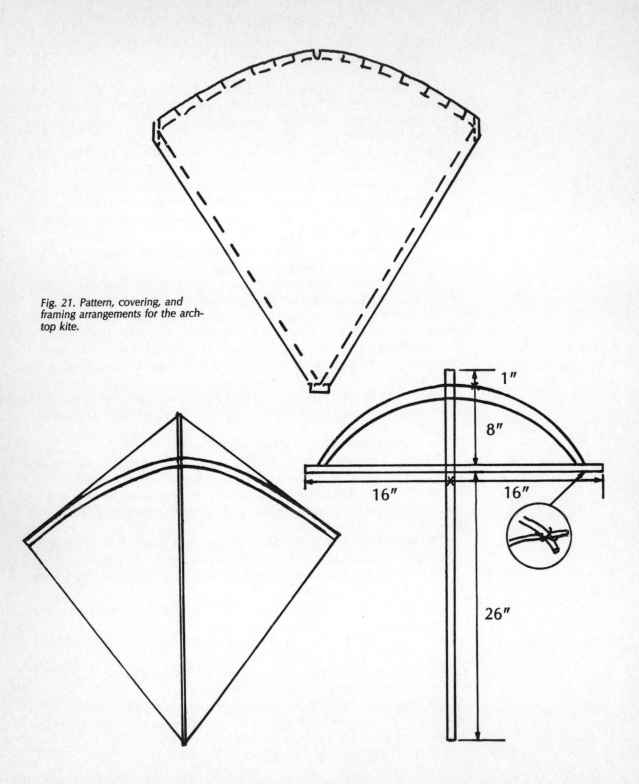

Fig. 21. Pattern, covering, and framing arrangements for the arch-top kite.

1"

8"

16"

16"

26"

❖ The other attachment is to the aft end of the longitudinal stick. Wrap the string around the end of the stick and pass it through the notch in the stick.

❖ The upper string should be about 24 inches long from the point of attachment to the bridle ring. The lower string is about 36 inches long.

❖ A single tail is usually used. Attach it to the aft end of the longitudinal stick.

**Variations.** You can construct the kite in a range of sizes with a variation of covering materials. Be sure to keep the proportions the same.

You can use other framing arrangements. Figure 22 shows some of them.

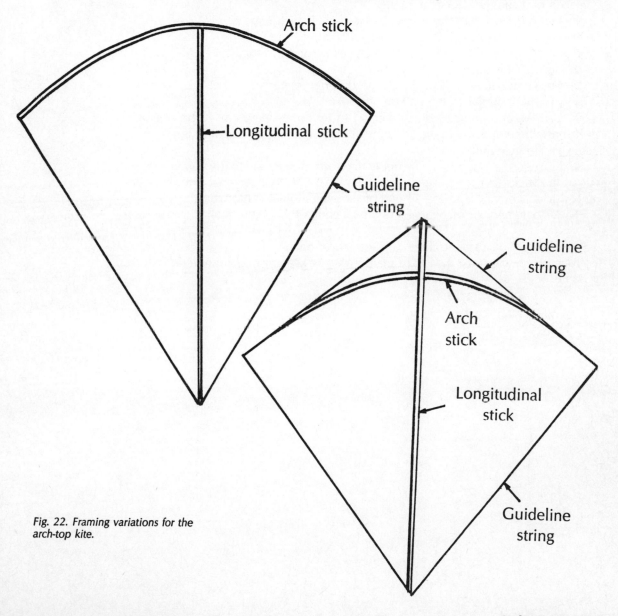

Arch stick

Longitudinal stick

Guideline string

Guideline string

Arch stick

Longitudinal stick

Guideline string

Fig. 22. Framing variations for the arch-top kite.

# OCTAGONAL KITE

The octagonal kite is usually used as a flat kite. It needs a tail.

❖ You need four 36-inch-long sticks for the frame. You can use either wooden sticks with a rectangular cross section of 3/16 × 5/16 inch, or round wooden dowels with a diameter of 3/16 inch.

❖ Cut a 3/8-inch notch at the ends of each stick. Make the notches on both ends of a stick in the same plane.

❖ Measure and mark the center point of each stick (Fig. 23).

❖ Glue and lash the sticks together with string.

❖ Install a guideline string in the notches around the sticks.

❖ Add lashing strings.

❖ Mark the pattern in Fig. 23 on the covering material.

❖ Cut the material to the pattern.

❖ Use the appropriate joining method to form the sleeves and hem.

❖ Install the material to the frame, with the guidelines passing through sleeves in the material.

❖ Use a four-string bridle. The upper three attachments are to the upper ends of the sticks that form the upper three corners of the octagonal form. The lower attachment is to the aft end of the longitudinal center stick.

❖ A single tail can be attached to the aft end of the longitudinal stick.

**Variations.** You can use three tails instead of one.

You also can construct the kite in a range of sizes, keeping the proportions the same.

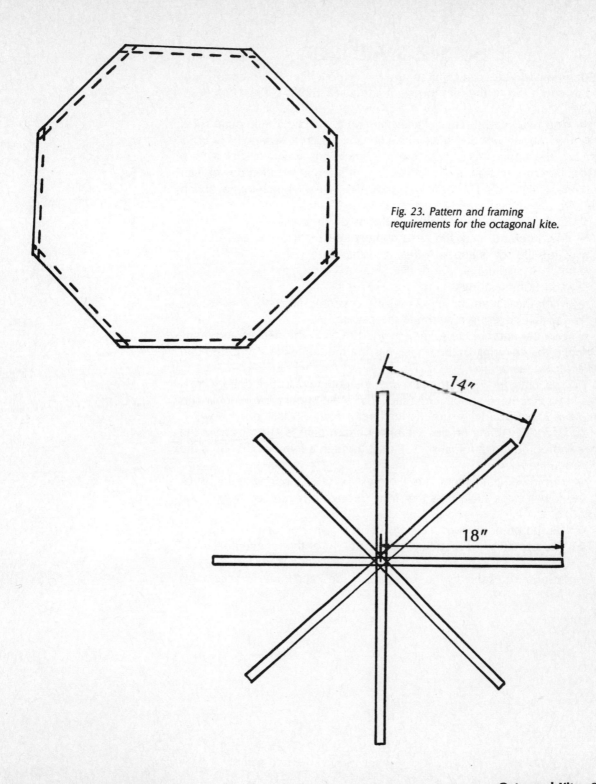

*Fig. 23. Pattern and framing requirements for the octagonal kite.*

14"

18"

# DOUBLE BASIC KITE

The double basic kite can be used as a flat or bow kite. You probably will need to add a tail to the kite to give it adequate stability.

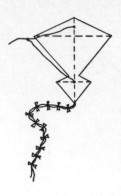

❖ You will need three sticks for the frame. For the longitudinal stick, use a 36-inch-long wooden stick with a rectangular cross section of ¼ × ⅜ inch. For the upper cross stick, use a 32-inch-long wooden stick with a rectangular cross section of ³⁄₁₆ × ⁵⁄₁₆ inch, or a round wooden dowel with a diameter of ³⁄₁₆ inch. For the lower cross stick, use a 14-inch-long wooden stick with a rectangular cross section of ⅛ × ¼ inch.

❖ Cut a ⅜-inch-long notch in the ends of the sticks.

❖ Measure and mark the cross points of each stick (Fig. 24).

❖ Glue the sticks and lash them together with string.

❖ Use two guideline strings (Fig. 24).

❖ Add lashing strings.

❖ Mark the pattern in Fig. 24 on the covering material.

❖ Cut the covering material to the pattern.

❖ Use the appropriate joining method to form the sleeves and hem.

❖ Fit the covering to the frame, passing the guideline strings through sleeves in the material.

❖ You can add a bow string to either the upper cross stick or both cross sticks. If you are bowing both cross sticks, bow the upper stick 4 inches and the lower 2 inches. Make sure the longitudinal stick is inside the bow.

❖ Use a two-string bridle. The upper attachment is 4 inches from the upper end of the longitudinal stick. Pass it through a reinforced hole in the covering material.

❖ The lower attachment is to the cross point of the longitudinal stick and the lower cross stick. Pass the string through a reinforced hole in the covering.

❖ Tie the other ends of the strings to a plastic ring or in a loop.

❖ You can attach a single tail to the aft end of the longitudinal stick.

**Variations.** You can vary the sizes, proportions, and frame arrangements of this kite.

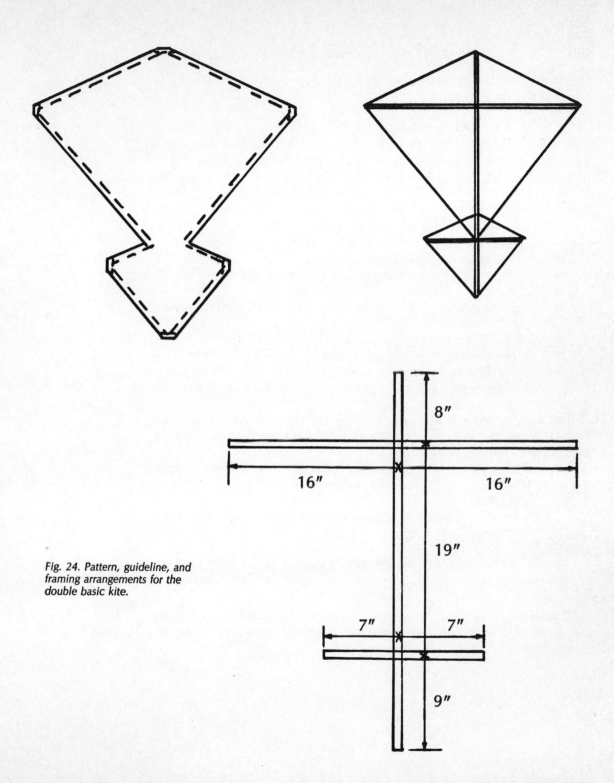

Fig. 24. Pattern, guideline, and
framing arrangements for the
double basic kite.

8"

16"                    16"

19"

7"        7"

9"

# DOUBLE SQUARE KITE

The double square kite can be used as a flat or bow kite. The kite often needs a tail for adequate stability.

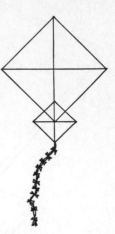

❖ You will need three sticks for the frame. For the 36-inch-long longitudinal stick, you need a wooden stick with a rectangular cross section of ¼ × ⅜ inch or a ¼-inch-round wooden dowel. The upper cross stick is a 30-inch-long wooden stick with a cross section of ³⁄₁₆ × ⁵⁄₁₆ inch or a ³⁄₁₆-inch-round wooden dowel. The lower cross stick is a 12-inch-long wooden stick with a ⅛-×-¼-inch cross section, or a ⅛-inch-round wooden dowel.

❖ Cut a ⅜-inch-deep notch in the ends of the stick.

❖ Measure and mark the cross points of each stick (Fig. 25).

❖ Glue the sticks and lash them together.

❖ Install two guideline strings in the notches around the sticks (Fig. 25).

❖ Add lashings.

❖ Use the lightest weight of covering material compatible with adequate strength.

❖ Mark the pattern in Fig. 25 on the covering material.

❖ Cut the covering material to the pattern.

❖ Join the material to form the sleeves and hem.

❖ Attach the covering material to the frame with the guideline strings passing through sleeves in the material.

❖ You can add a bow string to the upper cross stick only or to both cross sticks. The upper cross stick should be bowed 4 inches; the lower should be 2 inches.

❖ Use a two-string bridle. Make the upper attachment 6 inches from the upper end of the longitudinal stick, passing it through a reinforced hole in the covering material.

❖ The lower attachment is to the cross point of the longitudinal stick and the lower cross stick. It, too, passes through a reinforced hole in the covering.

❖ Tie the other ends of the strings in a loop or on a plastic ring.

❖ You can attach a single tail to the aft end of the longitudinal stick.

**Variations.** You can try a variety of kite sizes, keeping the proportions the same. You also can experiment with other proportions and frame arrangements.

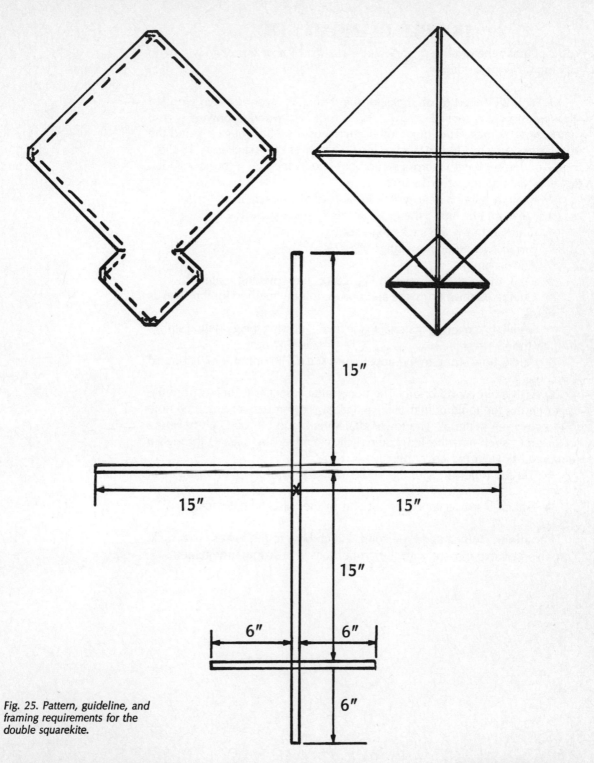

Fig. 25. Pattern, guideline, and framing requirements for the double square kite.

# DOUBLE DIAMOND KITE

You can make the double diamond kite as a flat or bow kite. You will need a tail for adequate stability.

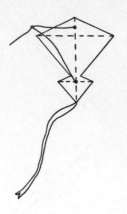

❖ You will need three sticks for the frame. You can use two wooden sticks with a cross section of ¼ × ⅜ inch or two wooden dowels with a diameter of ¼ inch. The longitudinal stick must be 36 inches long and the upper cross stick must be 30 inches long. The lower cross stick is an 18-inch-long wooden stick with a cross section of ⅛ × ¼ inch, or a round wooden dowel with a diameter of ⅛ inch.

❖ Make a ⅜-inch-deep notch in both ends of each stick.

❖ Measure and mark the cross points of each stick (Fig. 26).

❖ Glue and lash the sticks together.

❖ Install two guideline strings (Fig. 26).

❖ Add lashings.

❖ Mark the pattern shown in Fig. 26 on the covering material.

❖ Cut the pattern, using the appropriate joining method for the sleeves and hems.

❖ Install the covering material to the frame, passing the guideline strings through the sleeves.

❖ Add a bow string to the upper cross stick. The upper stick is bowed 4 inches.

❖ Use a two-string bridle. The upper attachment is 6 inches from the upper end of the longitudinal stick, and is passed through a reinforced hole in the covering material. The lower attachment is to the cross point of the lower cross stick and the longitudinal stick, and is also passed through a reinforced hole in the covering.

❖ Tie the other ends of the bridle strings to a small plastic ring or in a loop.

❖ Attach a single tail to the aft end of the longitudinal stick.

**Variations.** You can add a second, 2-inch bow to the lower cross stick. You also can experiment with the proportions and frame arrangements.

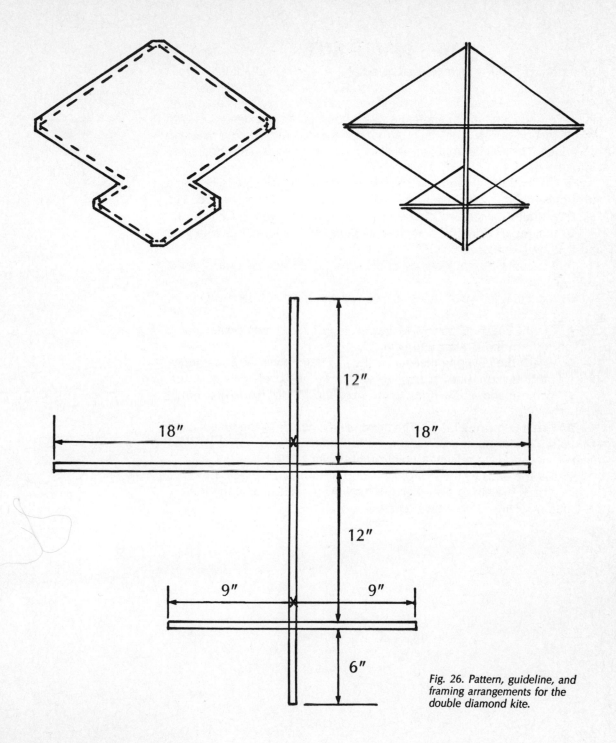

Fig. 26. Pattern, guideline, and framing arrangements for the double diamond kite.

# FOUR-CIRCLE KITE

The four-circle kite is usually used as a flat kite. It requires a tail.

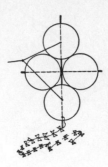

❖ The frame consists of a longitudinal stick, a cross stick, and four circle sticks. For the longitudinal and cross sticks, you can use wooden sticks with a cross section of ³⁄₁₆ × ⁵⁄₁₆ inch or round wooden dowels with a diameter of ³⁄₁₆ inch. The longitudinal stick is 32 inches long; the cross stick is 24 inches long.

❖ To form the circles, use 36-inch lengths of ⅛-inch square or round strips of bamboo. Each circle should have a diameter of 11 inches. (See Fig. 27. Techniques for forming circles from bamboo are given in Chapter 2.)

❖ Join the longitudinal and cross sticks at their center points with glue and a string lashing.

❖ Assemble the four circles to the cross frame with glue and string lashings (Fig. 27).

❖ Mark the circle pattern in Fig. 27 on the covering material. Four circles are required.

❖ Cut the covering material to the pattern, using the appropriate joining method to form the sleeves and hem.

❖ Attach the covering material to the kite frame over the circle frame sticks, with the sticks passing through sleeves in the cover.

❖ You can add a bow string to the cross stick, if desired. Use a 4-inch bow.

❖ Use a two-string bridle. The upper attachment is to the longitudinal stick at the center point of the upper circle. The lower attachment is to the longitudinal stick at the center point of the lower circle.

❖ Tie the ends of the strings in a loop or to a small plastic ring.

❖ Attach the tail to the aft end of the longitudinal stick at the joint of the bottom section of the lower circle.

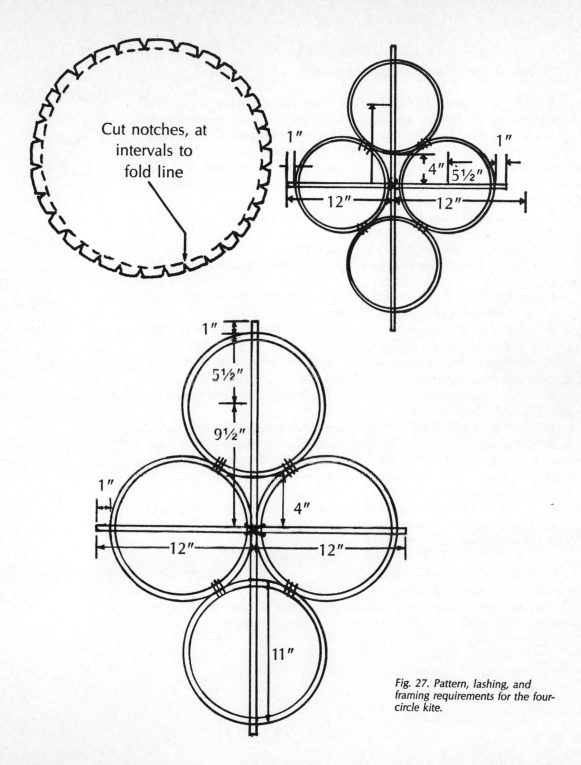

Cut notches, at intervals to fold line

1"

4"

5½"

12"

12"

1"

1"

5½"

9½"

1"

4"

12"

12"

11"

Fig. 27. Pattern, lashing, and framing requirements for the four-circle kite.

# TRIPLE-DECK KITE

The triple-deck kite is usually used as a flat kite. A tail is needed.

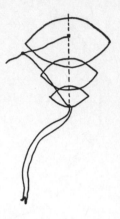

❖ The frame pattern for the triple-deck kite is shown in Fig. 28. For the 36-inch-long longitudinal stick, use a ¼-×-⅜-inch rectangular wooden stick or a ¼-inch-diameter wooden dowel. For the arch sticks, use bamboo sticks or ³⁄₁₆-inch-diameter wooden dowels. You need two sticks 36 inches long for the upper form, two sticks 24 inches long for the middle form, and two sticks 16 inches long for the lower form. You can deviate somewhat from the cross-sectional measurements and still get satisfactory results.

❖ Measure and mark the points of attachment for the arch sticks on the longitudinal stick (Fig. 28).

❖ Mark the center point on each arch stick.

❖ Glue and lash the arch sticks to the longitudinal stick, following the pattern.

❖ Bend and join the ends of the arch sticks with glue and string lashings ½ inch from the ends of the sticks to shape the three forms.

❖ Glue and lash the arch sticks together where the forms overlap Fig. 28.

❖ Mark the pattern shown in Fig. 28 on the covering material. Notice that three separate cover pieces are used, with open spaces left between forms.

❖ Cut the covering material to the patterns, using the appropriate joining method to form the sleeves and hems.

❖ Attach the cover to the kite frame, forming sleeves over the arch sticks.

❖ Use a two-string bridle. The upper attachment is to the longitudinal stick at the center point of the upper arch form. The lower attachment is to the aft end of the longitudinal stick at the point where the lower arch stick joins the longitudinal stick.

❖ Tie the other ends of the strings in a loop or to a small plastic ring.

❖ Attach a single tail to the aft end of the longitudinal stick at the joint of the lower arch stick.

**Variations.** You can add bow strings to the arch sticks if you prefer. Bow the sticks to the size you desire.

You can experiment by changing the relative sizes and shapes of the forms. A kite with two decks and four decks or more are possibilities.

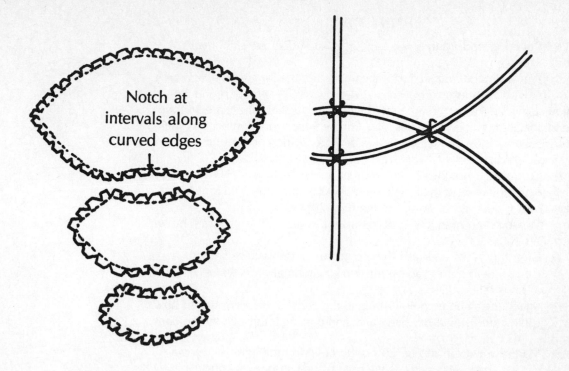

Notch at
intervals along
curved edges

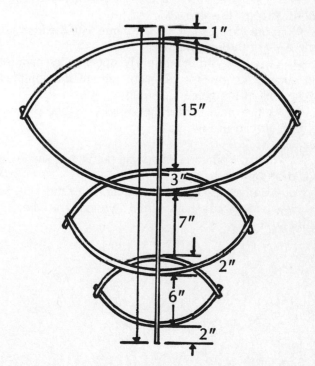

1"

15"

3"

7"

2"

6"

2"

Fig. 28. Pattern, lashing, and
framing requirements for the triple
deck kite.

# BIRD KITE

You will need to add a tail to give the bird kite adequate stability.

❖ You will need four sticks for the frame. For the longitudinal and arch sticks, use wooden sticks with a ³⁄₁₆-×-⁵⁄₁₆-inch cross section or round wooden dowels with a ³⁄₁₆-inch diameter. The two longitudinal sticks are 30 inches long; the arch stick is 36 inches long. For the 9-inch-long lower cross stick, use a wooden stick with a cross section of ⅛ × ¼ inch or a round wooden dowel with a diameter of ⅛ inch.

❖ Cut ⅜-inch notches in the ends of the arch stick.

❖ Taper the ends of the longitudinal sticks at the upper end for a V joint and make a groove for a string lashing (Fig. 29).

❖ Measure and mark the cross points for joints on the sticks as shown in Fig. 29.

❖ Glue the sticks and lash them together to the pattern shown.

❖ Tie a guideline string across the two longitudinal sticks 19 inches from the upper ends (Fig. 30).

❖ Attach the same guideline string to the ends of the arch stick to bow it by wrapping the string around the stick and passing it through the notches (Fig. 30).

❖ Mark the pattern in Fig. 29 on the covering material.

❖ Cut the covering material to the pattern and use the appropriate joining method to form the sleeves.

❖ Install the cover to the kite frame with the frame sticks and guideline string passing through sleeves.

❖ Use a three-string bridle. The upper attachment is to the center of the arch stick. The lower attachments are to the longitudinal sticks at the attachments of the guideline string.

❖ Tie the other end of the strings in a loop or to a small plastic ring.

❖ You can use two tails.

**Variations.** You can use a wide tail with a single attachment (Fig. 30) instead of the two-tail arrangement.

You also can use other constructions for this kite. Some flat or bowed bird kites have heads shaped from Styrofoam or other lightweight material.

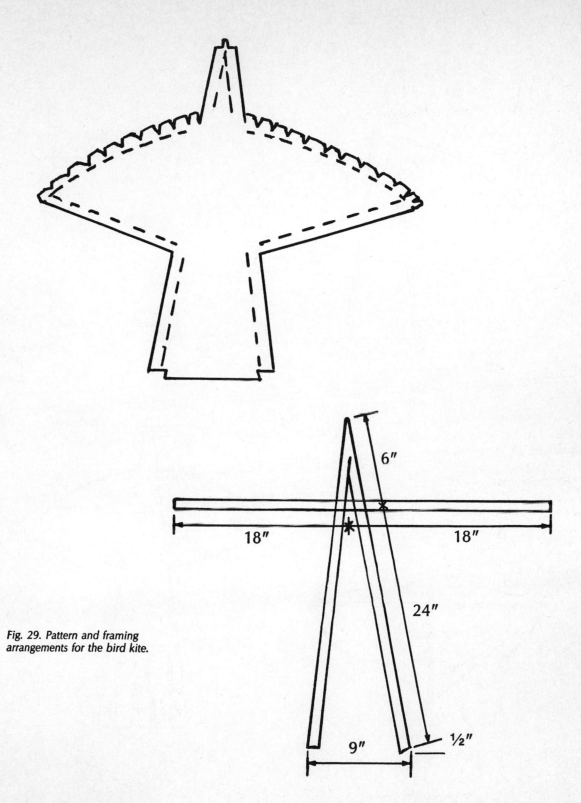

Fig. 29. Pattern and framing arrangements for the bird kite.

6"

18"          18"

24"

9"          ½"

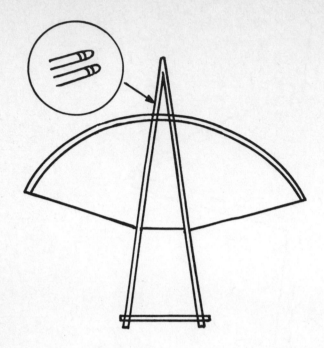

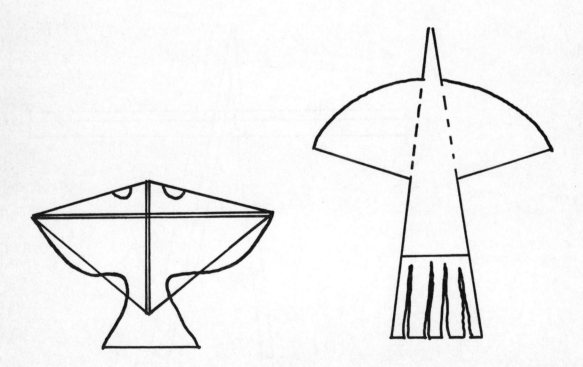

Fig. 30. Guideline requirements and covering variations for the bird kite.

# DRAGON OR SERPENT KITE

A long, wide tail is usually used on this type of kite.

❖ Three sticks are used to make the frame. For the longitudinal and cross sticks, use wooden sticks with a cross section of ³⁄₁₆ × ⁵⁄₁₆ inch or round wooden dowels with a diameter of ³⁄₁₆ inch. The longitudinal stick is 16 inches long and the cross stick is 18 inches long. You can use a 36-inch-long strip of bamboo for the curved stick.

❖ Mark the patterns for the joints on the sticks (Fig. 31).

❖ Assemble the sticks, as shown in Fig. 31, gluing and lashing the joints with string.

❖ Attach a guideline string between the lower end of the longitudinal stick and the ends of the curved stick.

❖ Mark the pattern in Fig. 31 on the covering material.

❖ Cut the covering material to the pattern, using the appropriate joining method to form the sleeves and hem.

❖ Attach the covering material to the frame, with the frame sticks passing through sleeves in the material.

❖ If the tail is an extension of the covering material, attach a separate sleeve to it over the guideline string.

❖ Use a two-string bridle. The upper attachment is to the longitudinal stick where the curved stick is attached to it. The lower attachment is to the aft end of the longitudinal stick where the guideline string is tied.

❖ Tie the other ends of the strings in a loop or to a small plastic ring.

❖ The tail is usually an extension of the covering material or a separate piece of material that is attached to the lower portion of the covering material. You can use wide and extremely long tails, even those 30 feet or more in length. The tails usually taper.

**Variations.** You can use longitudinal sticks from 1 foot or less in length to 3 feet or more by keeping the proportions the same. A variety of other arrangements are possible, such as those in Fig. 32.

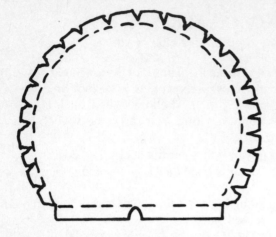

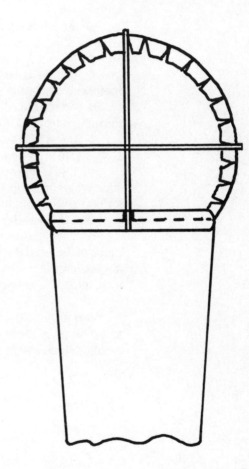

Fig. 31. Pattern, framing, and covering requirements for the dragon or serpent kite.

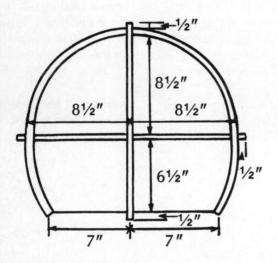

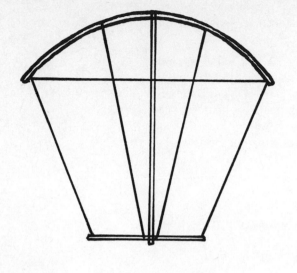

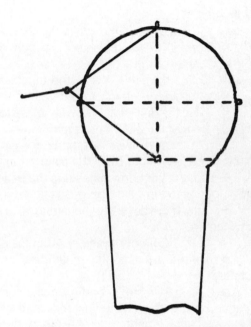

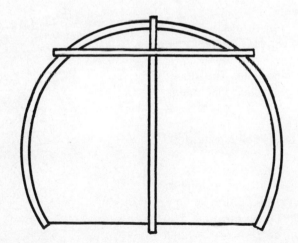

Fig. 32. Framing variations and
bridle requirements for the dragon
or serpent kite.

# CENTIPEDE OR CATERPILLAR KITE

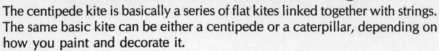

The centipede kite is basically a series of flat kites linked together with strings. The same basic kite can be either a centipede or a caterpillar, depending on how you paint and decorate it.

❖ Eight separate ring frames are required. Each frame is the same and requires three sticks. You can use bamboo sticks. It is important to have the frames as light in weight as possible. Therefore, you will need to use bamboo strips that have the smallest cross-sectional size compatible with adequate strength.

❖ The longitudinal and cross sticks are 15 inches long. For the 12-inch-diameter circle, you will need a 40-inch-long stick.

❖ To make a frame, mark the center point on both the longitudinal and cross stick (Fig. 33).

❖ Glue and bind the sticks together.

❖ Form a 12-inch-diameter circle from the 40-inch-long strip. (Directions are in Chapter 2.)

❖ Splice the ends of the strip together as shown in Fig. 33.

❖ Glue the joint and lash it with string.

❖ Glue the ring and lash it with strings to the longitudinal and cross sticks.

❖ Repeat for the other seven frames.

❖ A separate cover is required for each frame. You can use different colors for each frame. Mark the pattern in Fig. 33 on the covering material.

❖ Cut the covering material to the pattern, using the appropriate method of joining to form the sleeves and hems. Repeat for the other seven frames.

❖ Attach the covers to the frames with the circle sticks passing through the sleeves.

❖ Link the frames together 10 inches apart, on four strings.

❖ Tie the strings to the longitudinal and cross sticks outside the circle frames.

❖ Use a two-string bridle on the forward, or face, kite. The upper attachment is to the longitudinal stick above the upper circle stick attachment; the lower attachment is to the longitudinal stick below the circle stick attachment.

❖ Tie the other ends of the strings in a loop or to a small plastic ring.

❖ You can add a single tail to the last circle form.

**Variations.** Instead of one tail, you can add small decorative tails or streamers to the ends of the cross sticks of each frame (Fig. 33).

You can use circles 6 inches or less in diameter to 3 feet or more. You also can vary the number of frames you use. Keep in mind, however, that the more rings you use the more difficult it will be to fly the kite.

A popular variation uses progressively smaller ring diameters to form the kite. Another choice is to place the rings progressively closer together. This method works well when progressively smaller rings are also used.

You can use long cross sticks with the ends extending well beyond the edges of the rings. You can extend the longitudinal sticks in the same way.

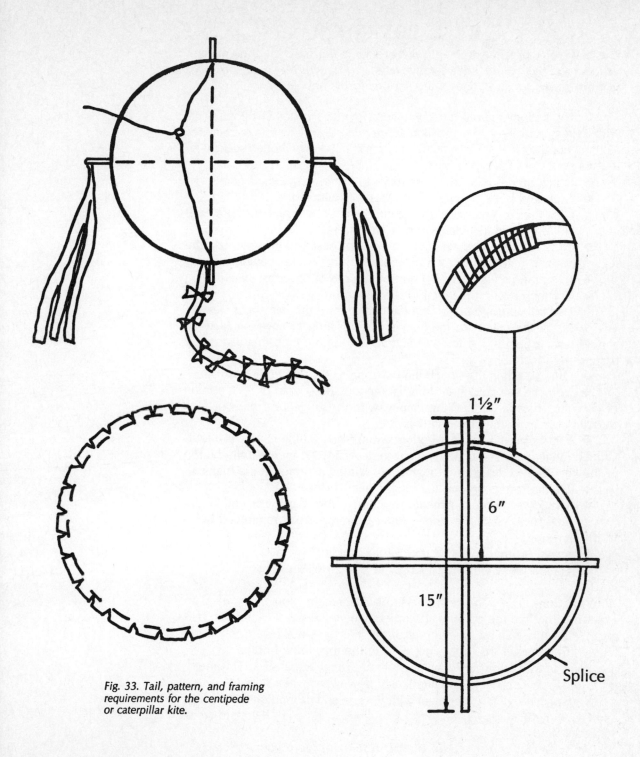

Fig. 33. Tail, pattern, and framing requirements for the centipede or caterpillar kite.

1½"

6"

15"

Splice

# BASIC BOX KITE

The basic box kite is extremely popular and is the basis for a number of variations of the cellular kites detailed later. The basic box kite can be flown without a tail, which is one of the reasons for its popularity.

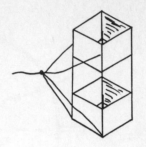

❖  For the longitudinal sticks, you need four 36-inch-long wooden sticks with a cross section of ¼ × ⅜ inch, or wooden dowels with a diameter of ¼ inch. For the cross sticks, you need four 17-inch-long wooden sticks with a cross section of ³⁄₁₆ × ½ inch.

❖  Notch the ends of the cross sticks to fit the longitudinal sticks.

❖  Glue and bind the cross sticks together with string.

❖  Glue the cross frames to the longitudinal sticks 5½ inches from each end of the longitudinal sticks as shown in Fig. 34.

❖  You will need two separate covers. For best performance, use the lightest weight material that is compatible with adequate strength.

❖  Mark the pattern (Fig. 34) on both pieces of covering material.

❖  Cut the covering material to the pattern lines.

❖  Use the appropriate joining method to form the hems and sleaves.

❖  Install the covers to the frames. Each section of covering material should have a hem at the top and bottom and form a loop that fits snugly around the longitudinal sticks.

❖  Glue or otherwise attach the covering to the longitudinal sticks.

❖  You can use guideline strings at the top and bottom of each section of covering material around the frames, with the guideline strings passing through sleeves in the covering (Fig. 34).

❖  You can use a variety of bridle arrangements. One choice is a four-string arrangement. The upper two attachments are 5½ inches from the top of the kite. The strings pass through small reinforced holes in the material.

❖  Tie the strings around the longitudinal sticks.

❖  The lower two attachments are 1 inch from the lower end of the longitudinal sticks, with the strings passing through small reinforced holes in the covering.

❖  Again, tie the strings around the longitudinal sticks.

❖  Tie the loose ends in a loop or to a small plastic ring.

**Variations.** You can use a one-string attachment. You might need to experiment to find the point of attachment where the kite flies in good balance. With this method, one corner of the kite faces downward when the kite is flown, rather than one side, as with the four-string bridle.

You can try a two-string attachment to one longitudinal stick. This method also has one corner of the kite facing downward when flown.

You might want to experiment with the size and proportions of the kite, such as wider or narrower sections of covering or different length-to-cross-sectional ratios.

You also can construct box kites with three or more box sections.

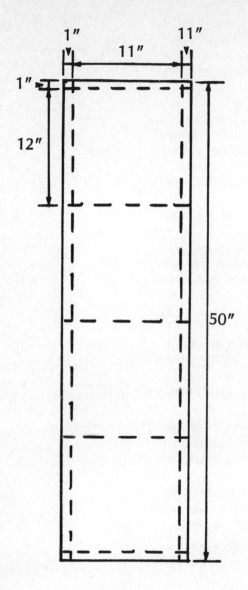

1″    11″    11″

1″

12″

50″

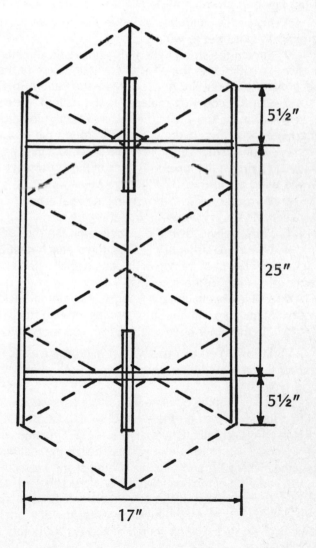

Fig. 34. Pattern, framing, and guideline arrangements for the basic box kite.

5½″

25″

5½″

17″

# BOX KITE WITH SIDE WINGS

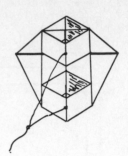

A box kite with side wings combines features of both the basic two-stick flat kite and the basic box kite. This kite is usually flown without a tail.

❖ Construction of the frame is basically the same as for the basic box kite. An exception is the addition of the cross stick for the wings, which is a 36-inch-long wooden stick with a cross section of ¼ × ⅜ inch or a ¼-inch-diameter wooden dowel.

❖ Notch the ends of the longitudinal sticks in the wing plane.

❖ Make a ⅜-inch cut in each end of the cross stick in the wing plane.

❖ Glue the cross stick and lash it with strings to the longitudinal sticks just below the upper covering material.

❖ Make a ⅜-inch cut in each end of the two longitudinal sticks in the wing plane in a direction parallel to the wing plane (Fig. 35).

❖ Install the guideline string in the notches in the ends of the sticks around the kite in the wing plane (Fig. 35).

❖ Stretch the string tight and tie the ends together with a square knot.

❖ In addition to the covering material used for the basic box kite, two sections of material are needed. Mark the pattern in Fig. 35 on them.

❖ Cut the covering material to the pattern lines.

❖ Form the sleeves in the material for the longitudinal sticks and join the material to the covering material around the box frames.

❖ To attach the wing covers to the kite, join the upper and lower sections to the covering at the top and bottom of the kite along the longitudinal sticks in the wing plane (Fig. 3-5).

❖ Form sleeves in the covering material around the longitudinal sticks between the end covers.

❖ Form sleeves over the guideline on the outside edges of the wings.

❖ Use a two-string bridle. The upper attachment is to the longitudinal stick 5½ inches from the top of the kite, with the string passing through small reinforced holes in the covering.

❖ The lower attachment is to the longitudinal stick 5½ inches from the bottom of the kite, with the string passing through small holes in the covering.

❖ Tie the other ends of the strings in a loop or to a small plastic ring.

**Variations**. You can use two wing cross sticks. Construction is similar, except that the guideline string also passes through the notches on the second cross stick.

A variation of the box kite with single cross stick wings on one diagonal, is to add side wings on the other diagonal. Construction of the second set of side wings is basically the same as for the first side wings, with the second wing cross stick passing immediately below the first one. Join the two sticks together with glue and a string lashing at the crossing point.

A variation of the box kite with double cross stick wings on one diagonal is to add side wings on the other diagonal. Construction of the second set of side wings is basically the same as for the first side wings, with the two added cross sticks being joined at the center points with glue and string lashings.

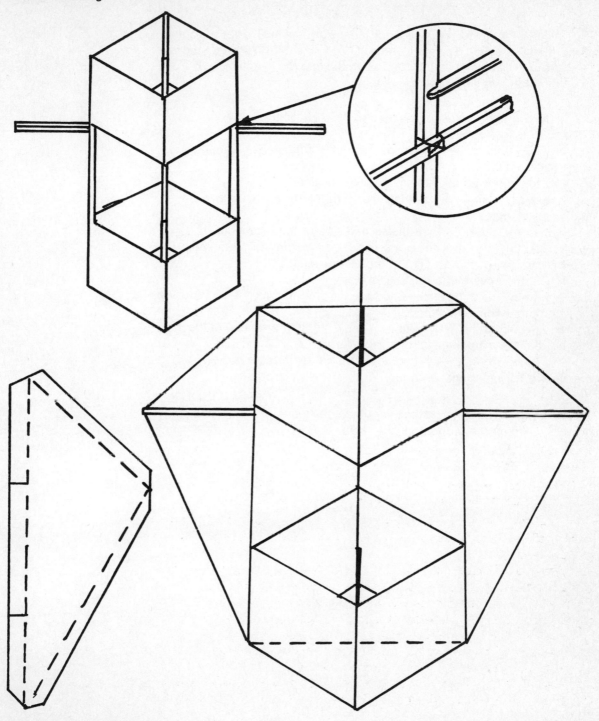

Fig. 35. Framing, pattern, and covering requirements for the box kite with side wings.

# SINGLE-UNIT TETRAHEDRON KITE

The single-unit tetrahedron kite is a true tetrahedron, with all sides and angles of the triangles equal. The structure is easy to assemble. All you need are six sticks of equal length, which you assemble into the tetrahedron. For use as a kite, only two sides are covered.

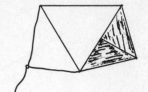

❖ To construct the frame, you need six ³⁄₁₆-inch-diameter wooden dowels that are 36 inches long.

❖ When joining the sticks, make all connections ½ inch from the ends of the sticks (Fig. 36).

❖ Glue and bind all joints with string lashings.

❖ Begin assembly by joining the ends of three sticks to form an equilateral triangle.

❖ Add two sticks to form the second side of the tetrahedron.

❖ Add the final stick to complete the construction of the frame.

❖ Mark the pattern in Fig. 36 on the covering.

❖ Cut the covering to the pattern lines.

❖ Join the covering material to form the sleeves over the sticks, using the appropriate joining method.

❖ Attach a bridle at two points. Tie the string to each end of the stick that has the covering material crossing over it.

❖ Tie the string at each end around the three joining sticks.

❖ Tie the other ends in a loop or to a small plastic ring.

**Variations.** You can construct the single-unit tetrahedron kite in a range of sizes, keeping the proportions the same.

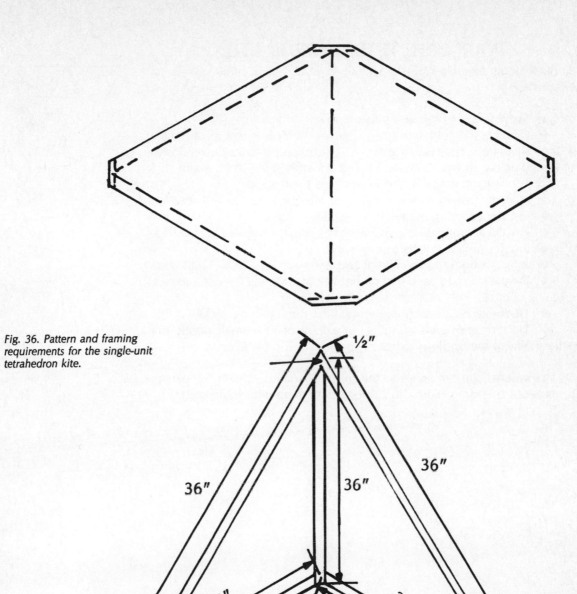

Fig. 36. Pattern and framing requirements for the single-unit tetrahedron kite.

½″

36″

36″

36″

36″

36″

36″

# FOUR-UNIT TETRAHEDRON KITE

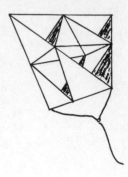

A four-unit tetrahedron kite is essentially a combination of four single-unit tetrahedron kites.

❖ Make four single-unit tetrahedron kite frames.

❖ Connect the guideline strings between the centers of all sticks (Fig. 37). An alternate method is to use twelve 18-inch-long wooden dowels instead of the guideline strings. Glue and lash them with string to the main sticks with the ends extending ½ inch beyond the main sticks.

❖ Mark the pattern shown in Fig. 37 on the covering. You will need four.

❖ Cut the covering material to the pattern lines.

❖ Use the appropriate joining method to form the sleeves over the sticks.

❖ Install the four covers to the frame.

❖ Attach a bridle to the kite at two points.

❖ Tie the string to each end of the stick that has the covering material crossing over it.

❖ Tie the string at each end around the three joining sticks.

❖ Tie the other ends of strings in a loop or to a small plastic ring. Adjustment of the bridle is extremely important for this kite.

**Variations**. You can construct the kite in a variation of sizes, keeping the proportions the same. You also can construct them with more cells.

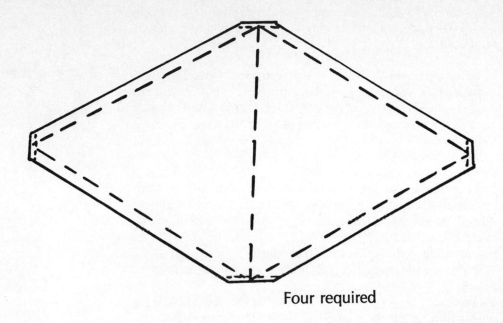

Four required

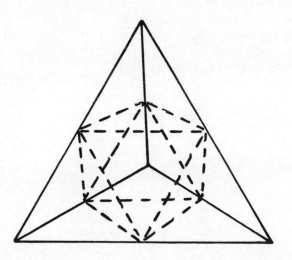

Fig. 37. Pattern and guideline requirements for the four-unit tetrahedron kite.

# DELTA WING KITE

A delta wing kite features a frame arrangement that allows considerable wing flexibility. A keel is used to give the kite stability, and the delta wing kite is usually flown without a tail.

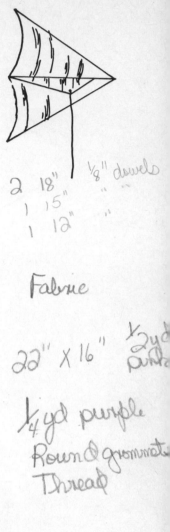

❖ For the frame you need ⅛-inch-diameter wooden dowels. The sticks at the outside edges of the wings are 18 inches long. Notice that they do not extend all the way to the forward tip of the kite. The center longitudinal stick is 15 inches long. The cross stick for the wings is 12 inches long. This stick is connected only loosely in pockets to the edges of the wings, and is not connected to the longitudinal sticks.

❖ Cut the sticks to the required lengths.

❖ You can use plastic film or cloth for the covering. You will need two pieces: one for the wing, and one for the keel. The pattern for plastic material, which will be glued or heat-sealed, and for the cloth fabric pattern, which will be sewn, are shown in Fig. 39.

❖ Cut the covering material to the pattern lines.

❖ Form the sleeves and hems, using the appropriate joining method for the material.

❖ Form sleeves or pockets for the sticks and join the keel to the wing materials. Construction details for plastic and cloth are shown in Fig. 39.

❖ Glue or sew the longitudinal center stick and the sticks at the outside edges of the wings in closed pockets.

❖ Form the pockets in the upper surface of the wings for the cross stick. An alternative is to use a wire hook on each end of the cross stick (Fig. 38), which is connected through small reinforced holes in the wing covering material, just inside the sticks along the edges of the wings.

❖ Make a hole in the keel for the attachment of the flying string. Reinforce it with tape, a small grommet, or other means.

**Variations.** You can construct the delta wing kite in a range of sizes, keeping the proportions the same.

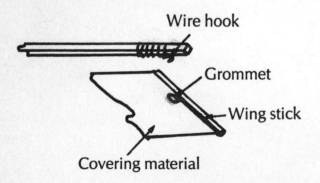

Wire hook

Grommet

Wing stick

Covering material

Fig. 38. Use of the wire hook and framing needs for the delta wing kite. See top of page 117.

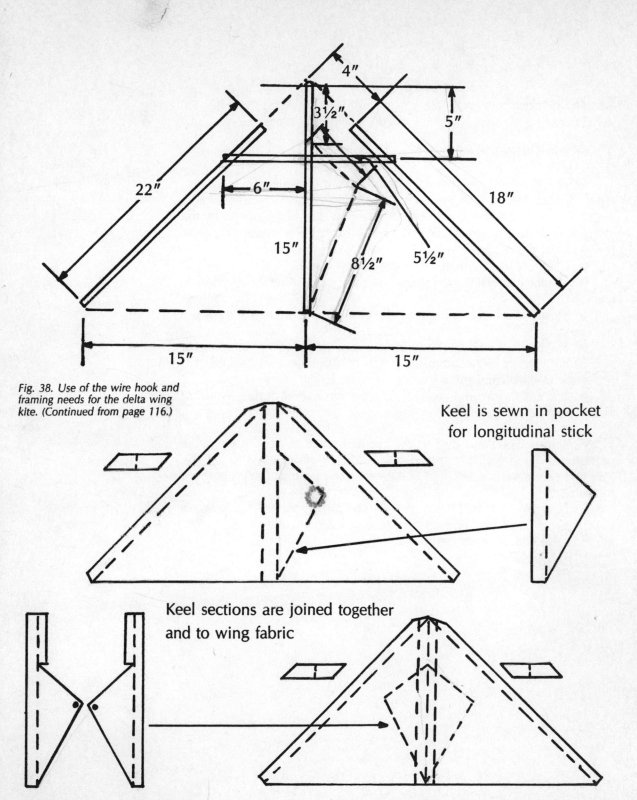

4"

3½"

5"

22"

6"

18"

15"

8½"

5½"

15"

15"

Fig. 38. Use of the wire hook and framing needs for the delta wing kite. (Continued from page 116.)

Keel is sewn in pocket for longitudinal stick

Keel sections are joined together and to wing fabric

# SLED KITE

The sled kite performs well and construction is easy. While sled kites are usually flown without a tail, you can add a tail if you prefer.

❖ You will need three 36-inch-long wooden dowels of ⅛-inch diameter for the sticks (Fig. 40).

❖ You can use thin plastic material or thin, flexible packing foam, especially Du Pont MicroFoam, as the covering material. One method is to use two layers of MicroFoam, joined in rows of welds, which allows for the insertion of sticks between the layers and makes construction extremely easy.

❖ Mark the pattern in Fig. 40 on the covering material.

❖ Cut the covering material to the pattern lines.

❖ Join the material to form sleeves over the sticks, using the appropriate method.

❖ Make holes in the covering for the bridle strings. Reinforce the holes with tape.

❖ The bridle has two points of attachment. Tie the strings in a loop or to a bridle ring 72 inches from the points of attachment to the kite. It is important to have each string exactly the same length.

❖ You can use a tail if desired. You can join a short decorative tail of plastic to the aft edge of the covering material.

**Variations.** You can construct the kite in a range of sizes, keeping the proportions the same. Another variation is the two-stick design in Fig. 40. You also can make this variation in different sizes, keeping the proportions the same.

For both two- and three-stick variations, you can experiment with changes in the basic proportions and with the size and placement of the air vent. You also can use two or more vents.

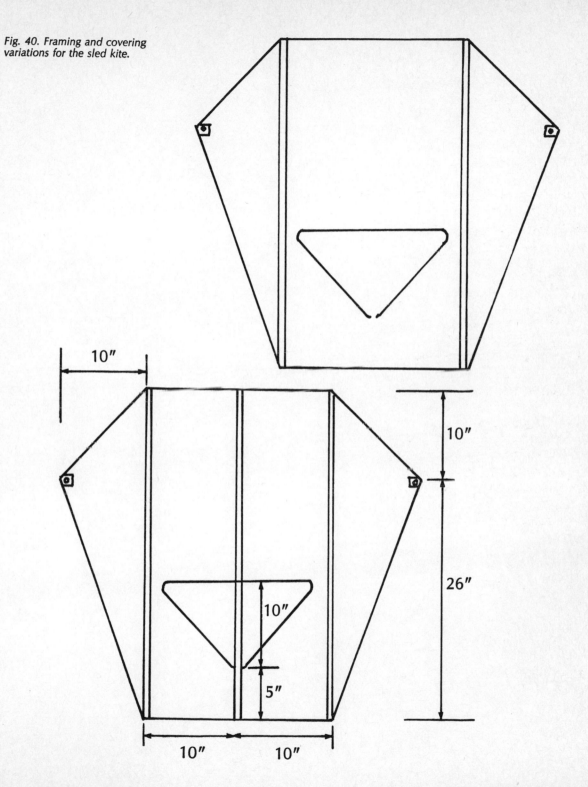

Fig. 40. Framing and covering variations for the sled kite.

10″

10″

26″

10″

10″

5″

10″

10″

# Index

# Index

# Other Bestsellers From TAB

☐ **FRAMES AND FRAMING: THE ULTIMATE ILLUS-TRATED HOW-TO-DO-IT GUIDE—Gerald F. Laird and Louise Meiére Dunn, CPF**

This illustrated step-by-step guide gives complete instructions and helpful illustrations on how to cut mats, choose materials, and achieve attractively framed art. Filled with photographs and eight pages of full color, this book shows why a frame's purpose is to enhance, support, and protect the artwork, and never call attention to itself. You can learn how to make a beautiful frame that complements artwork. In this clear concise reference, the authors describe for you the procedures involved in picture framing. 208 pp., 264 illus., 8 pages full color.

**Paper $12.95**             **Hard $19.95**
**Book No. 2909**

☐ **STRIP QUILTING—Diane Wold**

Diane Wold is an expert quilt-maker and her enthusiasm for the art of strip quilting is contagious. After introducing you to the tools, fabrics, techniques, and sewing methods used in strip quilting, she covers all the steps needed to complete a finished project including making borders, backing, using batting, basting, doing the actual quilting, and binding. You'll also find directions for using different types of patterns—multiple bands, one-band shifted patterns, and more. 184 pp., 165 illus., with 8 Full-Color Pages.

**Paper $12.95**             **Hard $21.95**
**Book No. 2822**

☐ **DEMYSTIFYING COMPACT DISCS: A GUIDE TO DIGITAL AUDIO—Daniel Sweeney**

This time- and money-saving sourcebook will guide you in finding the CD player and accessories that meets your needs for the best possible price. The strengths and weaknesses of this new medium are carefully examined along with tips on how to get the best performance, available accessories and even a look at the future of digital audio. 176 pp., 83 illus.

**Paper $9.95**             **Book No. 2728**

☐ **CANVAS AND UPHOLSTERY PROJECTS FOR BOATS AND RVs—Jack Wiley**

This easy-to-follow guide to modern canvas and upholstery techniques for boats and RVs thoroughly covers everything you need to know to do a professional job . . . from the tools needed to the basic hand sewing stitches such as herringbone, round stitch, and slip stitch . . . from the materials you'll need and where to get them, to operating, choosing, and repairing a heavy-duty upholstery machine. 320 pp., 327 illus.

**Paper $15.95**             **Book No. 2719**

☐ **BUILD YOUR OWN KIT HOUSE—Jonathan Erickson**

Building a house from a kit is an affordable choice. Erickson makes it possible for you to buy and build a kit home of your own from scratch. It answers real-life questions potential kit homeowners should pose to lending institutions, contractors, dealers, and others. The pros and cons of time, cost, and quality are examined so that you can make decisions from a solid knowledge base. 272 pp., 153 illus.

**Paper $14.95**             **Hard $22.95**
**Book No. 2873**

☐ **FARMSTEAD MAGAZINE'S GUIDE TO ANIMAL HUSBANDRY—Editors of *Farmstead* Magazine**

Here's a gold mine of information for homesteaders raising a single cow or goat for their own use . . . or the small farmer using his animals as a source of income. Just some of the other topics covered in this incredibly comprehensive sourcebook include: beekeeping, raising rabbits for fun and profit, how to buy and care for a horse, and the tricks of raising guinea birds, even advice on controlling insect pests. 168 pp., 20 illus.

**Paper $9.95**             **Hard $15.95**
**Book No. 2764**

☐ **BUILD YOUR OWN WORKING FIBEROPTIC, IN-FRARED AND LASER SPACE-AGE PROJECTS—Robert E. Iannini**

Here are plans for a variety of useful electronic and scientific devices, including a high sensitivity laser light detector and a high voltage laboratory generator (useful in all sorts of laser, plasma ion, and particle applications as well as for lighting displays and special effects). And that's just the beginning of the exciting space age technology that you'll be able to put to work! 288 pp., 198 illus.

**Paper $15.95**             **Hard $24.95**
**Book No. 2724**

☐ **BUILDING METAL LOCATORS: A TREASURE HUN-TER'S PROJECT BOOK—Charles D. Rakes**

With the metal detectors you'll build using this project guide, you'll be ready to get started in a hobby that is challenging and potentially PROFITABLE! Detectors covered include: frequency-shift metal locators, a simple beat frequency oscillator, balanced inductance locators, transmitter/receiver circuits, a VLF coin searcher, and a VLF deep searching locator! 126 pp., 102 illus.

**Paper $9.95**             **Hard $15.95**
**Book No. 2706**

# Other Bestsellers From TAB

□ **BEGINNING BLACKSMITHING, WITH PROJECTS—Jim Converse**

This illustration-packed handbook includes everything from a history of blacksmithing to traditional blacksmithing techniques. Jim Converse explains types of welds, how to heat a piece of iron, where to buy a forge and anvil, and how to set up and maintain a small shop. The projects included will teach you, hands-on, all the fundamentals of blacksmithing. 288 pp., 260 illus.

**Paper $12.95**      **Hard $18.95**

**Book No. 2651**

□ **COSMOLOGY: THE SEARCH FOR THE ORDER OF THE UNIVERSE—Charles J. Caes**

Was there really a "Big Bang" that created our universe? How many stars exist in the universe at any one moment? These are just a few of the many mysteries of our universe that are explored in this tantalizing look at man's ongoing search for an understanding of cosmic order. This is a selection that none interested in astronomy, cosmology, cosmogony, or astrology should miss! 192 pp., 24 illus.

**Paper $10.95**      **Hard $16.95**

**Book No. 2626**

□ **THE METALWORKER'S BENCHTOP REFERENCE MANUAL—Joseph W. Serafin**

This one-stop, ready reference contains all the information and instructions on metalworking that you need to complete any metalworking endeavor. By illustrating new approaches and unusual machining methods it will help you solve practically any metalworking problem you encounter. The ideal answer book for anyone interested in the craft of metalworking, as well as for those in the profession, this all-encompassing sourcebook covers techniques for working with all types of metals. Packed with illustrations to ensure absolute understanding! 320 pp., 360 illus.

**Paper $16.95**      **Hard $25.95**

**Book No. 2605**

□ **THE DARKROOM BUILDER'S HANDBOOK—Carl Hausman and Stephen DiRado**

Have your own fully equipped home darkroom for a fraction of the price you'd expect to pay! Picking from the darkroom examples in this book, you'll be able to design a "dream" darkroom that meets your own specific needs. Among the highlights: choosing a suitable location, equipment and accessories, even how you can make your home darkroom pay for itself! 192 pp., 238 illus.

**Paper $12.95**      **Book No. 1995**

□ **101 PROJECTS, PLANS AND IDEAS FOR THE HIGH-TECH HOUSEHOLD—Julie Knott and Dave Prochnow**

If you're looking for decorative effects, you'll be impressed with the number of ideas that have been included. Electronics hobbyists will be amazed at the array of projects included here—all of them with clear building instructions, schematics, and construction drawings. And you'll find exciting ways to use a microcomputer as a key decorative element in your high-tech atmosphere. 352 pp., 176 illus.

**Paper $16.95**      **Book No. 2642**

□ **PARTICLES IN NATURE: THE CHRONOLOGICAL DISCOVERY OF THE NEW PHYSICS—John H. Mauldin**

If you're interested in physics, science, astronomy, or natural history, you will find this presentation of the particle view of nature fascinating and informative, and entertaining. John Mauldin has done what few others science writers have been able to accomplish . . . he's reduced the complex concepts of particle physics to understanding terms and ideas. This enlightening guide makes particle physics seem less abstract—it shows significant spin-offs that have resulted from research done, and gives a glimpse of future research that promises to be of practical value to everyone. 304 pp., 169 illus., 16 Full-Color Pages, 14 Pages of Black & White Photos.

**Paper $16.95**      **Hard $23.95**

**Book No. 2616**

□ **101 THINGS TO DO WITH YOUR CAR—Editors of *School Shop* Magazine**

A treasury of practical do-it-yourself projects to enhance the performance and prolong the life of your car! This is a "tool" that belongs on every car owner's workbench. You'll find wealth of information to make you more knowledgeable about your car's modern transmission, fuel, electrical, exhaust, and other systems—know-how that may save you money when you need to take your car to a garage for more major repairs. 160 pp., 160 illus.

**Paper $9.95**      **Hard $15.95**

**Book No. 2073**

□ **WORKING WITH ACRYLIC PLASTICS, Including 77 Projects—Jack Wiley**

Learn to make practical and attractive items out of plastic—an inexpensive and readily available material that is amazingly simple to work with. Now with these easy-to-follow instructions and show-how illustrations, you can learn to create all kinds of useful and decorative items from acrylic—home accessories, gifts, jewelry, art, furniture, dishes, and more! 256 pp., 328 illus.

**Paper $11.95**      **Hard $18.95**

**Book No. 1959**

# Other Bestsellers From TAB

☐ **MAKING KNIVES AND TOOLS—2nd Edition—Percy W. Blandford**

Here is the completely revised and expanded new second edition of a guidebook that has become the "bible" in its field. Written by a highly respected metalworking/woodworking craftsman, it shows you how you can make almost any type of edged tool or knife, at amazingly affordable cost! You'll learn how to make pro-quality knives and tools from plain kitchen knives to shaping tools. 256 pp., 187 illus.

**Paper $12.95**  **Hard $18.95**
**Book No. 1944**

☐ **TIME GATE: HURTLING BACKWARD THROUGH HISTORY—Charles R. Pellegrino**

Taking a new approach to time travel, this totally fascinating history of life on Earth transports you backward from today's modern world through the very beginnings of man's existence. Interwoven with stories and anecdotes, and illustrated with exceptional drawings and photographs, this is history as it should always have been written! It will have you spellbound from first page to last! 288 pp., 142 illus.

**Paper $16.95**  **Book No. 1863**

☐ **333 SCIENCE TRICKS AND EXPERIMENTS—Robert J. Brown**

Here is a delightful collection of experiments and "tricks" that demonstrate a variety of well-known, and not so well-known, scientific principles and illusions. Find tricks based on inertia, momentum, and sound projects based on biology, water surface tension, gravity and centrifugal force, heat, and light. Every experiment is easy to understand and construct . . . using ordinary household items. 208 pp., 189 illus.

**Paper $9.95**  **Hard $15.95**
**Book No. 1825**

☐ **COMETS, METEORS AND ASTEROIDS—HOW THEY AFFECT EARTH—Gibilisco**

Information on meteors, asteroids, and other related space phenomena is all here for the taking. It includes a spectacular eight-page section of color photos taken in space. Packed with little-known details and fascinating theories covering history's most memorable comets—including Halley's Comet—the origins of the solar system, and speculation on what may happen in the future. 224 pp., 148 illus.

**Paper $14.95**  **Book No. 1905**

☐ **333 *MORE* SCIENCE TRICKS AND EXPERIMENTS—Robert J. Brown**

Here's an ideal way to introduce youngsters of all ages to the wonders and complexities of science . . . a collection of tricks and experiments that can be accomplished with ordinary tools and materials. You can demonstrate that air is "elastic," perform hydrotropism, or psychological tricks . . . or perform any one of more than 300 fascinating experiments. 240 pp., 213 illus.

**Paper $10.95**  **Hard $15.95**
**Book No. 1835**

☐ **EMERGENCY LIGHTING AND POWER PROJECTS—Rudolf F. Graf and Calvin R. Graf**

Literally packed with practical advice and how-to-be-prepared solutions, this is a handbook every homeowner should have! You'll find a wealth of information on energy-efficient lighting, security systems for home and business, tips on commercially available products for home and camp power generation, plus a wide range of easy-to-construct and highly useful power projects! 384 pp., 130 illus.

**Hard $18.95**  **Book No. 1788**

*Prices subject to change without notice.

**Look for these and other TAB books at your local bookstore.**

**TAB BOOKS Inc.**
**Blue Ridge Summit, PA 17294-0850**

**Send for FREE TAB Catalog describing over 1200 current titles in print.**
OR CALL TOLL-FREE TODAY:  **1-800-233-1128**
IN PENNSYLVANIA AND ALASKA, CALL:  **717-794-2191**